A
WEALTH
OF
WISDOM

A WEALTH OF WISDOM

Legendary African American Elders Speak

EDITED BY

Camille O. Cosby and Renee Poussaint

FULL-PAGE PORTRAITS BY

Howard L. Bingham

WASHINGTON SQUARE PRESS

New York London Toronto Sydney

W Washington Square Press
1230 Avenue of the Americas
New York, NY 10020

ISBN-13: 978-0-7434-7892-2

ISBN-13: 978-0-7434-8229-5 (Pbk)

First Washington Square Press trade paperback edition February 2007

10 9 8 7 6 5 4 3 2

Designed by Laura Lindgren

WASHINGTON SQUARE PRESS and colophon are
registered trademarks of Simon & Schuster, Inc.

Manufactured in the United States of America

For information regarding special discounts for bulk purchases,
please contact Simon & Schuster Special Sales at 1-800-456-6798
or business@simonandschuster.com.

Thank you, Visionaries, for showing us how

ACKNOWLEDGMENTS

We want to extend our deepest thanks to all those who labored long and hard to make this book a reality. First, of course, to each of the wonderful visionaries who opened their homes to us and shared their stories. Also, to our Visionary Heritage Fellows, the college students who worked so hard to introduce us to the extraordinary elders from their local communities. You will learn more about each of them as you move through the book.

The logistics of pulling a book together with so many varied elements can be a major challenge. We could not have met that challenge without the unwavering determination of two central members of our small staff: Doug Spiro, our project director; and Nicole McGee, our education director. Thanks in that area also go to Joel Brokaw, Sondra Pugh, and Terri Revis.

The book might not have made it beyond the proposal stage were it not for our board member and veteran author, Dr. Ray Winbush, and our skilled representative Manie Barron, who steered us through the many hurdles with warmth, humor, and a firm belief in the project.

Our thanks, of course, also go to Judith Curr, the publisher of Atria Books, and Senior Editor Malaika Adero. They shared our enthusiasm for the book from the very beginning and helped us through the initial painful stages of having to select excerpts from the full, rich interviews we had done with each of the National Visionaries.

ACKNOWLEDGMENTS

The power of the book comes not only from the elders' words but from their faces. We are extremely pleased that veteran photographer Howard L. Bingham agreed to create the vivid photographic portraits included herein.

Finally, we want to thank our families for sharing our passion and commitment not only for this book but for the elders who continue to show us the way.

CONTENTS

CONTENTS

PREFACE

It is difficult to realize how much has changed since *A Wealth of Wisdom: Legendary African American Elders Speak* was first published in 2004. We were pleasantly surprised when it climbed to number 21 on the *New York Times* bestseller list. But most important, we were, and continue to be, touched and energized by the readers' responses, the personal stories you've shared of wonderful elders who've shaped your lives.

We've had glimpses of painful memories from America's segregated past: a grandmother's story of how it felt to be good enough to be hired to raise a person's child, but not good enough to come through that person's front door, or a great-uncle's willingness to finally talk about fighting for his country overseas in World War II, and facing his country's continuing racism when he got home.

We've laughed at shared family rituals, like being sent outside as a child in the country to find the right small-sized branch or "switch" to be used by the adult who would spank you, or the fact that every adult in the neighborhood would know and share with your mother the details of any mischief you might have gotten into well before you made it home.

We've heard so many of you talk about being inspired to record your own elders' stories, not only in your family, but in your churches and neighborhoods. You've shared with us your concerns that so many of these stories are being lost as families change, many church congregations dwindle, and historic downtown African American communities disappear under the economic force of gentrification. Many of you have said that you want to keep these stories for your children as a legacy of their family's and their people's strength. You've said that you want to let the children see the proud shoulders on which they stand and, hopefully, understand that their young lives are too valuable to waste through self-destructive mistakes.

Unfortunately, we continue to be struck by how little many of our children really know about that rich legacy, and some of them point the finger of blame squarely at the adults who helped raise them. They complain that in their families, the adults often wanted to protect the children from the painful Jim Crow realities of the past and would not talk about their lives or their struggles against racism.

They also said that their neighborhoods offered few alternative sources for them to hear these stories, since most of these young people grew up in modern communities where the generations are often isolated from each other. They have no sense of the old extended-family neighborhoods, where access to elders and their stories of guidance were an everyday part of growing up and understanding who you are and who you could become.

In school, their access to this invaluable material was often no better. These days, their frustrated teachers complain to us that under the most recent government guidelines, they are only able to "teach for the test," with no time for the kind of individual stories that could bring our country's history truly alive for their students.

All of this has reinforced our understanding of how vital *A Wealth of Wisdom* really is, as well as the organization behind it, the National Visionary Leadership Project. We are first and foremost an intergenerational, educational organization. Our goal continues to be to "ensure that the lessons learned from our country's African American elders are preserved and passed on to the young people who will be the leaders of tomorrow." We do this through recording lengthy videotaped interviews with extraordinary elders, teaching college students to do similar comprehensive interviews of elders in their own local communities, and, finally, using the latest modern technology to distribute this invaluable material. This multilayered work of the National Visionary Leadership Project constitutes *one of the few strategies left for documenting the truth about human history.*

Since the book's original publication in 2004, we have continued to record these wonderful interviews with both famous and little-known elders. Our collection is now well past the two hundred mark. We've expanded the scope of our website (www.visionaryproject.org) to include more interview excerpts, as well as the full webcasts of intergenerational roundtables with legendary visionaries such as Ruby Dee. We were particularly pleased to have the National Educational Association note the value of NVLP's website as an educational resource in its monthly magazine sent to more than 3.2 million teachers.

We've expanded the number of college students and universities in our Visionary Heritage Fellows Program, focusing on the stories of local community elders. We've inaugurated programs with local high schools, helping students to capture the often inspirational stories of their school's graduates, and the close-knit black communities that nurtured them. We launched a highly successful essay contest and a series of visits by our visionaries to local high schools. We're now exploring ways to work with elementary school students as well.

We're looking forward to our next Intergenerational Summit on the State of Black America, a dialogue across generations on current issues, held each year in partnership with the Library of Congress. The participating visionaries honored at our most recent summit included Leah Chase, Joycelyn Elders, Rachel Robinson, Bill Russell, Sonia Sanchez, Percy Sutton, and Wyatt T. Walker.

We are particularly pleased that our ongoing partnership with the Library of Congress has now expanded to include the protection and preservation of NVLP's original master tapes in the library's permanent archive.

As a means of responding to all of you who've asked for help in recording your own elders' stories, we've created our *Legacy Guide,* available on our website. It takes families and community groups not only through the process of interviewing their elders, but also through the fun of creating local events (dinners, school plays, etc.) based on their stories. We've set up a new website, the National Registry of African American Oral Histories, to collect information on the location of the large numbers of invaluable existing audio- and videotapes, held not only in museums and university libraries, but also in people's homes and attic boxes.

We're exploring the possibilities of television documentaries and a children's series. We've also been gathering material for another book, a new collection of excerpts from those visionaries we've interviewed since the original *A Wealth of Wisdom* was published.

In the final analysis, however, we've long known that the most important priority must be making this history accessible to our young people as early and as often as possible. That means getting it into classrooms across the country so that teachers can bring it to their students as a core part of the regular curriculum. Understandably, this is not an easy task, but we are pleased to say that in the fall of 2006 we took a major step. After months of preparation, revisions, and testing, NVLP launched a groundbreaking web-based lesson plan on the Civil Rights Movement, using the faces and voices of our visionaries, the people who lived through and often led that movement.

Since *A Wealth of Wisdom* was published in 2004, the urgency of our mission has been painfully reinforced, as we lost, one after another, some of the wonderful elders who shared their memories with us in the book. With that pain has come some of the joy of being able to keep their works, their faces, the inimitable expressions, and sounds of their voices with us, vibrant and strong, and immediately accessible through the NVLP website and other initiatives.

These extraordinary men and women were kind enough to share their lives with us so that we and our children can continue to learn and grow and build on their phenomenal foundation. What a gift! How pleased we are to be able to continue to share it, and how grateful we are to each and every one of them, whose lives we will forever celebrate.

—Dr. Camille O. Cosby and Renee Poussaint

Visionaries, in This Edition, Who Have Passed Away
As of September 15, 2006

Keter Betts
Renowned jazz bassist, educator

Ray Charles
Singer, musician, composer

Shirley Chisholm
First African American woman elected to the U.S. Congress; first woman
to seek a major party nomination for the presidency of the United States

Ossie Davis
Actor, civil rights activist, screenwriter, director

Katherine Dunham
Choreographer, dancer, writer

Samuel Gravely
Retired admiral, United States Navy

Marcus Gunter
Educator, musician

John H. Johnson
Founder of *Ebony* and *Jet* magazines, publisher, corporate executive

Coretta Scott King
Civil rights leader

Constance Baker Motley
First African American woman appointed to the federal judiciary,
former New York state senator

Gordon Parks
Photographer, author, poet, filmmaker, composer

INTRODUCTION

One of the most wonderful and consistently frustrating parts of being a television journalist for so many years was finding myself constantly rushing back to the station midafternoon to get my report ready for the six o'clock news, excited about some fascinating person I'd just interviewed and all of the lengthy stories and invaluable insights captured on videotape, only to face the reality that all but a sliver of that material would end up on the figurative cutting-room floor. No one would be able to learn from them, be inspired by them. None of the young people, glued to their television sets, struggling, sometimes self-destructively, into adulthood, would benefit from these wise voices.

I lived in a world of varied, fascinating people and stories, but worked in a world of thirty-second sound bites. The contradictions were obvious. My precarious balancing act led to several Emmy Awards—and a bleeding ulcer.

What I really wanted was to do pretty much what I'd done growing up in Spanish Harlem; in Queens, New York; and in small Tennessee towns like Humboldt and Brownsville, where my maternal grandfather pastored a small church. I wanted to hear the elders' stories. On my mother's side, I wanted to hear about my great-grandmother, part Cherokee and tough as nails; about my late grandmother Gustava Maclin Vance, a pharmacist and the first African American woman to own a drugstore in her small, rigidly segregated town. I wanted to know how they survived the sometimes terrible hardships they faced.

On my father's side, I would sometimes plague my New York family with constant questions about where we came from. . . . How did we get the unusual name Poussaint? Why did our faces look so much like photos of strangers I'd seen in places like Mali and Martinique?

The elders in my family helped to fill in the blanks of who I was, by sharing stories of who and where I had come from. Those stories strengthened me in ways I am still discovering, by giving me a sense of the vast, rich African American foundation on which I stood.

What a wonderful gift! As a young girl, it made me want to hear about *other* people's stories, other cultures, other ways of thinking, acting, and responding to life's challenges. Each story was like the opening of a door to a new, unexpected vision of life. Each door gave answers to different questions, answers that meant there was no need to keep trying to reinvent the wheel; that a lot of the hard, fundamental work had already been done on some of society's (and my) contemporary problems. I did not have to start from the beginning. I could build on an existing foundation created by my elders.

I grew up wanting to share that gift with everyone. It seemed particularly important for some of the troubled young people I reported on, who kept making the same mistakes over and over again. They lived in a world where the different generations had little contact, where they and their young friends seemed to drift, often with no apparent moral compass. I continued to believe that if some of these kids could have consistent, open access to their elders' advice and life stories, it might make a difference, perhaps a small difference, but still something. This book and the National Visionary Leadership Project are the wonderful extensions of that lifelong belief.

When Camille Cosby and I joined forces to create NVLP, we agreed, first of all, that it had to be intergenerational. We needed to find ways to bring the elders and youth together on a consistent basis. We were driven by a real sense of urgency.

Some of the elders whose stories we wanted to capture on videotape were in their late eighties or early nineties. Some were younger, but battling health problems. They were the repositories of much of America's history in the twentieth century. Some of that history had never been shared beyond the confines of the black family, where the truth about their lives in a majority-white world could safely be told. Once those memories and stories were gone, that particular history could never be retrieved.

Some of the young people we wanted to reach, including those from solidly middle-class black backgrounds, were running headlong into various educational, social, and professional glass ceilings, unprepared for the remnants of racism that still plague our country. Some of them had no real sense of their heritage of struggle, and could not imagine life under segregation. They did not know what their elders had gone through to win the rights to the life they enjoyed, and for the most part felt little concern about protecting those hard-won victories—that is, until they themselves hit one of those glass ceilings. That lack of knowledge about their past made their futures vulnerable. Our aim in founding NVLP was to help by bringing the generations together for better, open communication about our shared history.

One thing that became abundantly clear as we interviewed these visionaries was that it's not possible to know an elder's *entire* story, but it's always fascinating to discover whatever we can. *A Wealth of Wisdom* gives glimpses of the visionaries' varied stories and experiences, a mix of the serious and the lighthearted.

We hope that young people, in particular, will see these elders as complex, complete individuals they can relate to—not icons, but vibrant individuals who laugh and cry, who've made mistakes, fallen down, but managed to get up and keep going, often with remarkable good humor.

We want young people to know these elders as children, much like themselves, being a feisty tomboy like Coretta Scott King or trying to imitate the dance moves of a cool older brother, like Geoffrey Holder.

We want them to know these figures as young adults on the front lines of the civil rights struggle, some of them facing constant violence, like Rev. Fred Shuttlesworth, who describes in this book the sound of the KKK bomb exploding at his family's home on Christmas Eve.

We want them to learn about long-term relationships, such as that of Ruby Dee and Ossie Davis as they talk frankly about the decades they spent trying to build a strong family, and the financial price they paid for refusing acting roles they could not be proud of.

Finally, we want everyone to see that in fact age *is* a very relative thing. These elders are shifting gears, not stopping. Katherine Dunham, at ninety-plus, a true grand dame of dance, still directs the occasional class. Carmen de Lavallade was recently photographed in fluid motion for a national fashion ad campaign. Now in his late eighties, Dr. John Hope Franklin is finishing a new book, and sharing vivid stories from a recent trip to the ancient city of Timbuktu, in Mali. And Dr. Dorothy Height, in her nineties, is still running the National Council of Negro Women, and traveling the country on a book tour for her new autobiography. And they are not alone.

These elders astound, exhaust, and inspire me. Hopefully, they will do the same for you.

—Renee Poussaint

We would like to thank each of the participating visionaries for allowing us to include excerpts from their videotaped interviews in this book.

In the context of our nonprofit organization, the National Visionary Leadership Project (NVLP), a "visionary" is defined broadly as an African American, seventy years of age or older, who has made a significant contribution in his or her field, and in the African American community.

Nominations are received from the public, and each year, the NVLP Board selects no more than thirty elders whose impact has been nationwide, known as *national* visionaries. Each national visionary sits for a lengthy videotaped interview in his or her home, done by either Camille Cosby or myself, the NVLP cofounders.

The interviews are transcribed, digitized, and permanently archived. A biographical Web page is created for each visionary, where video excerpts from the interview can be watched worldwide by the public on the NVLP Web site (www.visionaryproject.com). The original videotapes remain at the organization's Washington headquarters, where they are made available for scholarly research. Full transcripts are provided for the research libraries of partnering educational institutions.

The *local* visionaries are selected and interviewed by college students from their home communities, as part of our Visionary Heritage Fellows Program. No more than thirty fellows are selected each year from ten participating educational institutions, most of them historically black colleges and universities. Through an ongoing partnership between their schools and NVLP, the students receive intensive training in the areas necessary to complete a major research project and to conduct an interview with their chosen elder. Their faculty-supervised work is fully accredited as an independent-study course. After review, the NVLP Board chooses the top three student projects for scholarship awards.

These interviews of local visionaries by students are added to the NVLP archives, and as with the national visionaries, biographical Web pages and video excerpts are added to the Web site.

The interviews included in *A Wealth of Wisdom* were all done during NVLP's first year, 2002. Since then, the number of completed interviews has more than doubled. We hope to make a new *Wealth of Wisdom* book available each year, with excerpts included from the most recent group of visionaries.

The National Visionary Leadership Project is a nonprofit, 501c-3 organization. All proceeds from *A Wealth of Wisdom* will go to support and expand our educational and community outreach programs.

Our sincere thanks go to each and every one of the visionaries. They are extraordinary men and women, who've allowed us to share their historic experiences, wisdom, and life lessons to create an invaluable permanent legacy for generations of leaders to come.

For information on a variety of NVLP programs, and for video excerpts on each of the elders who are included in this book, please visit our Web site, www.visionaryproject.org, or call us at 202-331-2700.

—Renee Poussaint

A
WEALTH
OF
WISDOM

MAYA ANGELOU

Born in St. Louis, Missouri, on April 4, 1928

Poet, educator, historian, best-selling author, actress, playwright,

civil rights activist, producer, director

———— •◄ ►• ————

Maya Angelou is a remarkable Renaissance woman. She captivates audiences with her unique vigor, fire, and perception, and has the uncommon ability to shatter boundaries of race, gender, and class between reader and subject in a broad range of literary forms, both spoken and unspoken. She has authored numerous best-selling books, from I Know Why the Caged Bird Sings *to* A Song Flung Up to Heaven. *Films and plays in which she has appeared include such internationally acclaimed works as* Porgy and Bess *and* Roots. *Dr. Angelou made her directorial film debut with* Down in the Delta *in 1998 (Miramax Films).*

Throughout her career, Angelou has been showered with accolades, from a Tony Award nomination in 1973 to the Presidential Medal of Arts in 2000.

She has received more than forty honorary degrees, and in 1981 was appointed to a lifetime position as the first Reynolds Professor of American Studies at Wake Forest University. In January 1993, Angelou became only the second poet in U.S. history to have the honor of writing and reciting an original work at a presidential inauguration.

*M*any parents tell their children, either implicitly or explicitly, that they've never done anything wrong. "Oh, my goodness, if I had done that, my daddy would have killed me! Oh, no, I couldn't do that. That would hurt the family."

So, the young person thinks, my goodness, I must be the lowest thing in the world, because not only do I do that, I want to do it.

I wrote the book *Gather Together in My Name* to tell young people who've been told their parents have no skeletons in the closet that, in fact, they have no closets. I would admit where I've been, and they could see that, and realize that you may encounter many defeats but you must not be defeated. It may even be necessary to encounter the defeats, so you can know who you are, how you can rely upon yourself, where you can pull yourself up from.

Several years ago, I wrote about a very rough time I went through at eighteen. I went onto a national television show [years later], and the woman who interviewed me, who I knew slightly, said, "Maya Angelou, how does it feel to know you're the first black woman to have a national best-seller, nonfiction, and a second book nominated for the Pulitzer, and to know that at eighteen you were a prostitute?"

I had written the book, and just before I sent it out to the publisher, I called my mother, my brother, and my son. My husband had said, "Write it."

I had said, "People will hate me."

He said, "Write it if it's true. Young women and men, black, white, Asian, and Spanish-speaking have tried to reach an exit, and found the doors not only locked, but no doorknobs on the doors. It's important that you write it."

*The Maya Angelou Trio—publicity photo
from her career as a Calypso singer, ca. 1967–68*

So I called in the family and said, "There's a section you must know." And I read it to them. "If it's too painful, I'll take it out; but let me tell you why I want to write it."

My mom, as soon as I finished the section, stood up and said, "Is it ready for the post office? I'll take it myself."

And my brother, who is my heart, said, "You never have been a liar. I love you for it."

Of course, my heart is my son, who was in his twenties. He got up from the floor and came and sat beside me, and took me in his arms. He said, "You're great, Mother. You are great!"

On the book tour, I stopped in Cleveland, Ohio, to sign books. When *Gather Together* came out, department stores still had book sections in them! I was signing. The line was long, and suddenly there were two hands, black, young hands, with false fingernails. I followed the hands out; they led to false hair, lots of it, and to a young face, about eighteen, with false eyelashes.

It was ten o'clock in the morning.

She was a young street prostitute. She had heard me on television. She leaned over. She said, "You give me hope." Now, if no one else said anything to me, ever, that would be sufficient.

If you happen to be white in a white country; pretty according to the dictates of fashion; rich in a country where money is adored, it's almost impossible to grow up and to grow up honest inside. It is almost impossible. Most people don't grow up. Most people age. They find parking spaces, honor their credit cards, get married, have children, and call that maturity. What that is, is aging.

But to grow up, to take responsibility for the time you take up, and the space you occupy, to honor every living person for his or her humanity, *that* is to grow up.

I know what I've done. I mean, I've done it.

I'm on the board of lots of places, lots of universities. I teach all over the world and speak a lot of languages. But it's imperative that we not stand so upon the laurels. If you're firmly rooted in the ground, you're not so easily pushed over.

Most people don't grow up. Most people age. They find parking spaces, honor their credit cards, get married, have children, and call that maturity. What that is, is aging.

—MAYA ANGELOU

LEE ARCHER

Born in Yonkers, New York, on September 6, 1919

Tuskegee Airman, corporate executive

———◆———

Lee A. "Buddy" Archer served as a member of the distinguished Tuskegee Air-
men, a group who garnered an outstanding combat record in World War II.
Initially refused appointment to the U.S. Army Air Corps because he was
black, Archer went into the Army as a regular enlistee. In May 1942, while
stationed at Camp Wheeler, Georgia, Archer learned the Army Air Corps was
finally accepting black candidates for pilot training under the "Tuskegee
Experiment." He immediately reapplied.

In July 1943, Archer earned his wings and was commissioned as a second
lieutenant. He flew a total of 169 combat missions, including bomber cover,
convoy escort, scrambles, reconnaissance, and strafing, becoming the first
African American "flying ace." When he returned to the United States from
overseas, he became chief of the Instrument Instructors School, at Tuskegee
Army Air Field, in Alabama. Later selected for a regular commission, he went
to UCLA to complete his college education.

Archer retired after a twenty-nine-year career that included three CEO
positions in international military organizations. He had earned eighteen Air
Medals, the Distinguished Flying Cross, and Special Citations from presidents
Eisenhower, Kennedy, and Johnson, as well as the director of the CIA. He also

received the Accueil de Paris, an award presented by the mayor of Paris for activities in support of Franco-American relations.

My dad had two big rules. One: I'm your father, I make the rules. Two: you're my son, you obey them. And he took no foolishness about that. Another one of my father's rules involved his belief that kids get in serious trouble having three months of summer vacation with nothing to do.

My father [a successful businessman] had a house up in Saratoga Springs, New York, on a street called Congress Street. During the summer, while he continued to work in the city [the family lived for most of the year in Harlem], the rest of the family lived in that house at the top of a hill. I had a large group of very close friends on the street. As soon as school ended for the summer, my brother, Raymond, my sister, Harriet, and I went to Saratoga and stayed until school started again. My father's thinking was: "That's a great place because when I go visit the kids, there're horses there." By horses, he meant the Saratoga Springs racetrack; my father was quite a gambler.

(Incidentally, that Saratoga Springs neighborhood was technically integrated. In fact, if I remember correctly, we were the only African American family among Irish Americans. I spent every Saturday night at the YMCA. They had programs for youths. My brother and I were probably the only two African Americans in the program.)

At the end of Congress Street, there was a small private airport at which the wealthy racetrack people would arrive. I used to see these small air-planes come in and out, and I fell in love with them and wanted to fly. I took up reading about World War I, the flyers in World War I, the flying aces. That's when comic books had serious military slants. That was it! I decided I wanted to be a pilot. I was the original copy of Snoopy the dog in Charlie Brown: I saw aircraft; I loved them and the idea of flying.

My father, who had served in World War I, thought it was a loser's thing for an African American to participate in the war. He quoted *his* father, who had fought in the Spanish-American War, and told me, "You get no payment for it. Why are you going to do it?" One time my father even said, "Why don't you go to Canada and stay with your uncle? I'll send you a check each month."

I had made a decision that I wanted to fly in World War II. I didn't know about the rules and regulations that African Americans could never be in the Army Air Corps. The flying arm [of the U.S. Army] was part of the Signal Corps in those days. In 1925 the Army War College had done a study and concluded that African Americans, or "people of color," they said, could never learn to fly. They cited a number of reasons: we lacked courage, lacked the ability to fight in combat, were cowardly. They even said we lacked coordination! They must never have seen a basketball game or a track meet to make a ridiculous statement like that. Underlying all that was also the bias that no white man should ever have to take an order from a black man, a man of color. Well, they could have cut those other four reasons out and admitted, "This is the reason we don't want them in there." But they used subterfuge, as usual.

Without this knowledge, in 1940 a white friend and I decided we would join the Army Air Corps and go overseas to fight for our country. I was willing to fight for the country, to die for the country, despite its faults, warts and all. I knew I had to serve, not because the government wanted me to, but because I felt inside that I wanted to defend what was going to be the future of African Americans. I kept saying to myself, "If they'll do this to Jews, who are white, my God, what will they do to us?"

You can't tell me I can't do something. I'm a hardhead on that. I had an internal belief that I was good enough for the Air Corps. I was not compatible with being a servant in the military. They would have had a big problem out of me if I had not made it into flying school.

In 1942, after I had been in the service [Army] almost ten months, I was asked if I still wanted to go to the Army Air Corps, that it was going to be an experiment, the government's Tuskegee experiment. I said yes. They told me to report on the 25th of December 1942. When I saw the airplanes taking off and landing, the freedom of being up there at twenty thousand feet, above everything else, seemed romantic.

The military experience I had, good and bad, made me what I am. I've been rather successful—more in civilian life than I was in the military because there was a ceiling in 1970 when I left the service.

I went to work for General Foods as a manager with the assurance from a senior vice president that "You'll be given the shots and you'll be treated fairly." I became a manager of urban affairs. But in about seven or eight months, they discerned that I was not the happiest man in the world and asked me, "What would you like to do?"

I said, "I don't know." I knew nothing about being a civilian. But I said, "I'd like to do something more exciting or with the ability to move."

So they put me on the board of a venture capital company, Vanguard Capital Corporation. Months later, they relieved the president and asked me if I'd be president. The company sent me to the University of Pittsburgh to a program called Advanced Financial Management for Non-Financial Managers, a short course. I had no talent or background in finance. I could count, but that was it. I did very well, and came back and worked with the Minority Enterprise Mortgage Investment Corporation. After about a year, they transferred me as president to a larger business, Specialized Small Business Investment Company.

I hired a young lawyer, Reginald Lewis, who had come out of Harvard. I made him general counsel of North Street Capital Corporation, and with Ralph McNeal, who later became a city manager in Jersey, we were uniquely successful. Reginald Lewis later became the head of Beatrice International Foods.

During that period of about maybe twelve years, we financed seventy-four companies, including some of the biggest African American–owned companies in America, including *Essence* magazine, which recently sold a minority percentage for hundreds of millions of dollars; Rowley World Advertising Corporation; and *Black Enterprise*. [We had] also a helicopter company in Seattle that ended up being taken over by a big white company that services all of the companies that drill oil wells in the Gulf of Mexico.

Under the guidance of Reginald Lewis, Beatrice Foods became the largest black-owned business in America. In fact, of the one hundred largest black businesses, Beatrice International Foods is bigger than the other ninety-nine put together. We were very, very successful. Now I am the longest-serving member on the Beatrice board. Everyone else is gone, including Reg Lewis, who died suddenly.

It has been exciting because we now see African Americans at the head of major corporations—right now at three of the big ones, Time Warner,

American Express, and GE. The future is outstanding for these men—and there are women out there now who have tremendous jobs and potential prospects too. I even have a stockbroker now who is a young lady. At one time you didn't find any in the major brokerage firms.

There are women of color in the Air Force Academy, large numbers of them. And recently an African American woman became the first woman in the history of the military to become a commander of an active flying squadron. She's a commander of a tanker squadron in California. She's a rather small woman, I guess she's 5 foot 4 or 5. She flies the biggest airplane, the heaviest airplane, that the government makes. It's her job to get all those airplanes that she controls and all those pilots, who are mostly male, to fly wherever American bombers and fighters are, to do air-to-air refuelment.

I evaluate myself as a person first based on how my kids turned out. I have four children, three sons about three years apart and then a daughter ten years younger. I'm very proud of them. I think they're great people. They're much better people than I was at their age. Once, when I was a major and I had just come back from the Far East, my dad threatened to hit me upside the head if I hit my son Leon's butt again. Lee had run out into the street and I grabbed him, pulled him off his feet, and whacked the hell out of his bottom. My father said, "Buddy, if you hit that kid again, I'll break your neck." The guy who had these tough rules, who had threatened me with death at least once a month, suddenly tells me I can't even give my son a pat on the butt to teach him not to run in the street! We were walking down the street and out of the clear blue sky he turns to me and he says, "Buddy." "Yes," I say, wondering what it was going to be next. "I'm proud of you," he says.

I am *most* proud of the fact that I married someone I loved very, very much [Archer's late wife, Ina] and stayed married to her for fifty-two years without ever a thought of not being married to her, and that we raised four kids without them getting in trouble, yet.

I've done some other things that I'm very proud of, especially becoming a pilot. The only decoration I ever wear is sitting here on my shoulder: the command pilot wings. To become a command pilot took some doing under the conditions I faced.

We talk of this often when the older guys get together. We ask ourselves, who do we give it all to? Are they going to give something more to the young people coming behind them? And I'm confident that they will.

There's a lot of money out there for a lot of people. You have to be in there in the trenches with everyone else, fighting for your little piece.

Little by little [society is] changing. Not as fast as I would like it to. I would do it with a baseball bat: you *will* abide by the laws, you *will not* be racists. We have to be wary, keep our guard up.

I spent a lot of time in Germany. After talking to the Germans, I wondered how they could have been convinced to do the terrible things they did en masse. Despite the fact that all of them say, "I was never a Nazi," I say, "Well, who were those millions of people raising their hands hollering for the Führer?" African Americans have to be on guard all the time. And white Americans who don't complain [about racism] and who tolerate it, who say, "It's not my business that he's an SOB and acting that way," are as bad as the people who do it.

In 1985 I got a telephone call from Sam Poss, head of the Confederate Air Force [an organization dedicated to the preservation in flying condition of the great warplanes that dominated the skies during World War II].

Tuskegee Airman Lee Archer in the cockpit of his P-51 C, June, 1944

"Lee, could you get a couple of guys and come down to Houston for the Wings Over Houston air show?"

I snarled into the telephone, "Colonel Poss, why in the hell would I come to Houston, Texas, to anything called the Confederate Air Force for any reason whatsoever?"

"Well, we'd like to say that we're sorry about what happened in the past and that we've changed."

"Yeah, thank you," I said and hung up.

But then I thought about it, and I called him back up and said, "Hey, yes." I got Roscoe Brown, Spann Watson, and at our own expense, ten of us went down to Houston for the Wings Over Houston air show. "We'll go down there and we'll show these guys," we said. We were going to make a point.

It's a spectacular show, second biggest air show in America outside of Oshkosh. Once there, we found out they had dedicated the show to us, to the Tuskegee Airmen. That night they honored us at a big dinner, and Poss said to us, "Since I believe you find the word 'Confederate Air Force' offensive, although it was meant as a joke when they started the organization," he said, "we're going to make every effort to change the name." And they did.

[I'm] a street kid out of New York, but one of my father's mottoes was, "I brought you into this world and I'll take you out." So I could not join any gang or wear colors. The first time I wore a jacket with an insignia on it was as an Air Force pilot.

—LEE ARCHER

RUDOLPH BELISLE

Born in New Orleans, Louisiana, on March 17, 1932

Businessman, community activist, warden of Orleans Parish Prison

Selected and interviewed by
NVLP Fellow Byron Williams, Xavier University

———— ◆ ————

In his early life Rudolph Belisle enjoyed a career as an entrepreneur, owning and operating several clubs and convenience stores in New Orleans. He is now affectionately known as Chief Rudy or simply Chief. This title is well deserved; he obtained it working for the Orleans Parish Prison, where he has been employed for the past twenty-nine years. During this time, he has helped to diversify the leadership at the prison and has earned the respect of both colleagues and inmates. He is a respected member of Trinity Lutheran Church in New Orleans, where he participates in the men's ministry and uses his influence and personal finances to support outreach, tutoring, and recreational programs for youths and other members of the community.

I know the definition of poverty. When I graduated from high school, I didn't have a pair of shoes to wear to the ceremony. I was poor, very poor. A friend lent me his shoes. When I graduated from college, Mr. Henry, a friend of the family, sent me a suit and a pair of shoes to graduate in. I know what it means to be poor. I went many nights without food. I had some good friends, too. During the Christmas breaks, when I didn't have any money to come home, they would take me home with them.

I especially love the people in Alabama—they treated me as if I was a brother once I got married to my first wife. My mother-in-law and father-in-law treated me like their son, not their son-in-law. They were very, very, very good to me.

When I came back home, I did odd jobs to prove to my in-laws that I could make it even though I was poor. Everybody black was poor, not only me; times were hard then. We had to work.

Growing up, we had to cut wood. First you had to go find the wood; then you had to bring it home and cut it. We were fortunate because we lived on a corner that had a streetlight. You could cut wood at night. If my daddy came home and no wood was cut, he'd say, "Whose day was it to cut wood?" If it was your day, you got out there and cut that wood; you got out there at night and cut that wood. If you had to go find it, you found it.

My dad had a rule: he told my sisters, "You never leave the kitchen dirty, you never go to bed with your kitchen dirty, never." And you always cut your wood and got it in before bedtime. Everybody had woodstoves, and you had to clean the ashes out. We also had to keep house and clean the yard. Then you could play.

First you had to get your lessons; he demanded that you got your lessons. Then you had to do your chores. My two brothers and I split the days up to do these chores.

We eventually got a little property, and if people didn't have the money, my dad would let them stay there [for free]. He had communistic leanings, I think. The way he talked, if he were living nowadays, they'd probably put him in jail. They'd say he was a communist. He was smart. He could read and do mathematics. That's where I got it from. He could figure out problems.

He kept his family together. I never saw my father drink. I never saw my father hit my mother or cuss at her. I never heard him cuss in my life. Not one time did I ever hear my father cuss. He was a hard worker. Oh, he loved work. He'd come home from work and he'd want to do this and that.

I was lazy. I didn't like to work too much, at least not at the house, because I wasn't getting paid. I'd go *out* and work, you see. I'd cut grass all day—and we had a push lawn mower—where I could make $1.25, if I got a good customer. I'd be so tired. I'd take that money and buy a washing cake.

A washing cake was all the baker's leftover sweets mixed up together and baked. The cook would put a little pink icing on it, and [it would be] sold for a nickel. I'd buy a washing cake and a jumbo—a twenty-one-ounce milk—eat that, and, boy, I was full. I don't know how healthy it was for me, but I was full. I could sleep all day after that. But I couldn't sleep—that's one thing my mama didn't allow. While that sun shines, you're up.

When my father died, it took a lot out of me. I never did get to socialize with him, like I did with my mother, you know. My mother and I would sit down and talk all the time. When my mother was living, I always had somebody to talk to, even when I was a grown man. When I had marital problems, she used to call us together, and she'd listen and say, "Well, I'll tell you this . . ."

We used to have a little chimney—a fireplace—where we baked sweet potatoes. We'd sit there and she would tell us how her mama told her all about slavery; and how they used to work hard and pick cotton and different things. You see, her mother's mother was in slavery. She would tell us all kinds of old stories.

We used to sit around the table and eat together. We don't do that no more. I may eat at this television; somebody may eat at that television; someone eats in the kitchen. Most families don't know what a soup bowl is, or what it's like passing the bread, passing the meat. We don't sit down and eat and say a blessing and talk about what's going on.

If a problem comes up, we'll talk about it; but a long time ago, as poor as we were, we talked things out *before* a problem came up.

If you struggle from the beginning, you know what success is. I don't know if you can appreciate it if you have success all through life.

The thing that irritates me the most is when I see young black people who do not vote. They don't know the struggle we put up to vote. I don't care who you vote for, go vote. When I first went to vote, they asked me how many bubbles were in a bar of soap; and the fools talked at me about the Constitution. I knew more about the Constitution than all of them sitting in there. They told me to sign my name on a piece of Saran Wrap, then said, "You can't even write. Look where is your name!" That's the kind of thing we had to go through.

We had to go through all that to vote. We had to go back and come back and go back and come back again—but we fought to vote. I mean, people *died* to vote. But now you can go to the Phillips station to register to vote, and they [many young blacks] say, "Well, my vote ain't going to count, I ain't going." *Never* say your vote ain't going to count. I don't care who you vote for, go in there and cast your vote. People will respect you.

KETER BETTS

Born in Port Chester, New York, on July 22, 1928

Renowned jazz bassist, university instructor

Selected and interviewed by
NVLP Fellow Oliver Albertini, Georgetown University

World-renowned jazz bassist Keter Betts has played with some of the most important and influential names in jazz, including Dinah Washington, Charlie Byrd, Joe Williams, and Louie Bellson. He joined Ella Fitzgerald's band full-time in 1971 and performed with her for an unprecedented twenty-four-year stretch. Since making Washington, D.C., his home, Betts has continued with his music, while also devoting his energy toward teaching America's youth about music through lectures and workshops. He can be heard on more than one hundred jazz albums and has recently completed two self-released compact discs.

I love working with singers.

Each singer has their own particular style. Each one has their own fingerprints. And by having their own fingerprints, each one has their own voice prints. And so that's the difference.

It's the same for musicians. The fella at the drums, me at the bass, we aren't *playing* those instruments. The vibes player, he wasn't *playing* the vibes. He was playing himself, and coming through the vibes. And the drummer was playing himself, coming through the drums. What I'm thinking comes through my instrument.

I started playing drums in the fifth grade in my hometown, which was 80 percent Italian. My mother sent me to the store around the corner to get a loaf of bread and a bottle of milk. A parade came by, and when I came out of the store, I said, "What in the world is that!" I followed it all over town for about four hours. I got home, with the bottle of milk, the bread all crumbled, and my mother would have liked to kill me. But I explained that I followed this parade all over town. I said, "Mom, I want to play drums." So she got me a little snare drum.

There are two kinds of alarm clocks: the one that wakes you up any time in twenty-four hours; and another one that goes off inside your head and points you in the direction you're best suited for. I heard that second kind of alarm clock that day when I was in fifth grade and the parade came by.

If you hear that alarm clock, you start working in the direction that you're best suited for. Then you have to have a goal; you set the goal. It's like you're sailing on the sea of life, and you're the captain of your own ship. You're going to run into storms, and you might have to detour, you might have to alter your course. But you're still going toward your goal.

Either you become the captain of your own ship or you can be a rowboater. The rowboater has no ambition in life. Rowboaters get in a boat with no horsepower and drift along with the tide or have somebody else pull them along. They didn't hear an alarm clock, or don't know what a clock is.

This is my twenty-third year working with the Wolf Trap Foundation for the Performing Arts's Headstart program. For about eight years, I was doing music in over a hundred schools a year with the Washington Performing Arts Society's Concerts in Schools, in Prince Georges County and Montgomery County [Maryland]. Actually my purpose in doing that was to take kids around the world musically. I wanted to expose them to the music of the world, instead of what they get on television.

Even if a child is not going to be a musician, learning some type of music—piano, violin—instills discipline at a young age. Once they get that discipline, they can approach any subject. They have the built-in discipline.

Basically music is just discipline. In the beginning, all I wanted to do was get in the game, to get good enough to play. The first time somebody called me to play a job, I said, "Where is it?" Seven miles away. "Wow, I'm going seven miles and they're going to pay me!" Then, after a while, I started going after it, setting goals, and the next thing I knew, it got better and better and better. I was going down the road of life, or going on the sea of life, and it was rewarding.

Musicians are servants. We go around the world and play for people who don't speak any English. But we speak a language that they understand. We speak music. And that's the most important thing. They can understand, as I said before, that we're not playing an instrument, we're playing ourselves and coming through these instruments. Man, this is where you're *talking* to them. And they don't need an interpreter. The music doesn't need an interpreter.

When historians and archaeologists find ruins, they always find evidence of four things: art, music, literature, and dance. From the most advanced civilizations to the most primitive civilizations, they find those four things. This means that human beings have always wanted entertainment. To provide it, is a human gift.

Musicians are servants. We go around the world and play for people who don't speak any English. But we speak a language that they understand. We speak music.

—KETER BETTS

ADOLPHO A. BIRCH JR.

Born in Washington, D.C., on September 22, 1932

Tennessee Supreme Court Justice

Selected and interviewed by
NVLP Fellow Akeia Morris, Fisk University

———◆———

Adolpho A. Birch Jr. was the first African American to hold the office of Chief Justice of the Tennessee Supreme Court, serving in this capacity from May 16, 1996, through July 7, 1997. Over the course of his distinguished career he has also served on the faculties of Meharry Medical College, Fisk University, Tennessee State University, and Nashville School of Law. For his commitment and contributions to the practice of law, he has received numerous awards, including the Distinguished Alumnus Award from the Howard University School of Law.

*B*lack people in Washington, D.C., had their own or separate variety of everything. I never had to go to a segregated movie because there were movies right in the black neighborhood. We had a bank, stores—not department stores but grocery stores and such. Schools were segregated.

This segregation and atmosphere of segregation fostered some very, very good results in terms of education. There was just one academic high school for black students, and that was Dunbar High School. The colored part of the board of education put the best and the brightest teachers in that school. Most of them had Ph.D.s; all of them had studied their subjects profusely; they were all selected for academic excellence. The principal was a very fine man. Everybody was there to learn and go on to college. Nobody was there simply trying to get over, to do time and move on. It was truly an introduction to excellence.

The caliber of students was quite high. The curriculum was exemplary. I cannot say enough for the start that school gave me. Dunbar and Mott Elementary School stand out in my memory as two places of extreme significance in my life.

I never wanted to be anything else [other than a lawyer]. Racism and segregation merely increased my desire and hardened my resolve, but the initial desire was there in the first place.

All during law school, I had two jobs. I drove a taxicab, and I worked as a vendor at Griffith Stadium. I sold hot dogs for Redskins games, University of Maryland and Georgetown University football games, the Negro League games and Howard games, Washington Senators baseball games, and every event that came to Griffith Stadium, from Rosanna Tharp to Mahalia Jackson. On a good Redskins day, I could go home with $30 for two, two and a half hours worth of work, and still see the last quarter in the football game.

My father was the person I wanted to be most like as I was growing up. There were some people in my father's church I also looked up to. When I went away to college, though, I began to expand and look beyond family and immediate surroundings, to people like Frederick Douglass and Dory Miller, who was a World War II hero and Tuskegee Airman. When I got to law school, I narrowed it down to black lawyers, like Thurgood Marshall and Charles Hamilton Houston and William Hasty. They remained persons I admired greatly.

The continuing source of motivation was the sure knowledge that without a good education, I would not be able to contribute anything. Racism and segregation combined served as one of the best motivators because I knew they were wrong. I knew that there was no legal or moral basis for it. I felt it was mistreatment, an abuse of power, and I wanted to do all I could to help end it and make things equal or at least nonsegregated.

Along with every other black lawyer in Nashville, I provided legal representation for sit-iners who got arrested. I was a part of that legal team. There were eighty or ninety students and ten or fifteen black lawyers. We took turns.

I represented a young lady named Angeline Butler, a sit-iner from South Carolina who went to Fisk. I remember her name. Although she was one of many I represented, I remember her because her resolve has always stuck with me.

A highlight of my career was when I was able to watch James Nabrit, Thurgood Marshall, George Hayes, Louis Redding, and Louis Clymer as they rehearsed for their argument before the Supreme Court of the United States in the case of *Brown v. Board of Education of Topeka.*

J. Robert Bradley

Born in Memphis, Tennessee, on October 5, 1919

Gospel singer

Selected and interviewed by
NVLP Fellow T'Ebony Torain, Fisk University

———◆———

J. Robert Bradley is a world-renowned gospel singer and former director of music for the Sunday School publishing board of the National Baptist Convention. Throughout his tenure as a performer of the gospel genre, he has received numerous awards and honors, including being knighted Sir Robert Bradley by President William Tolbert of Liberia. Bradley has sung opera in Italy and France, classical music in London, and gospel on several continents. His melodic message has resonated with people of many nationalities, earning him global acclaim.

My mother was a great Christian. She used to tell people, "The Lord is gonna give me a man-child, and he's goin' be a servant of the Lord." And this has proven to be true. I hadn't gotten into this world as yet, but her word from the Lord has followed me all of my life. I have been in the church and working with church people all of my life.

I've been baptized twice. I was baptized in the Baptist church in Memphis, First Baptist Chelsea, which is still going, and I was baptized in Jerusalem, when I sang at the University of Jerusalem.

Church and the church people milk-fed me, as the old folks used to say. They took care of me and prayed for me. My mother was a strong prayer. She taught me how to pray.

I have spent my whole life praying and thanking God for his wonderful blessings, for he has brought me all these eighty-three years without a scratch, traveling by train, and on ships like the *Queen Elizabeth,* the *Ile de France,* the *Italiana,* and another great ship from Norway. I've traveled from Oslo, Norway, to Rio de Janeiro, Brazil, for the Baptist Youth World Alliance, where I served as soloist and guest soloist for attendees from every nation.

Yes, my mother was a praying woman. She wasn't an educated woman, but she had the spirit, and it was strong. She knew how to put the protection of God on you when it was necessary. Many times, when I would come home to Memphis after a trip, I would be asleep and I'd feel something rubbing my feet. I'd jump! It would be my mother praying, rubbing my feet, asking the Lord to rest my feet from a long trip.

Church people have always had me in their hands. Many fed me when I didn't have food at home. I know what it is to be hungry. I know what it is to need shoes. I know what it is to not have a house to live in, because they had set our little furniture out on the street because my mother couldn't pay the rent. I know what a hard time is.

The '30s were especially tough. The Great Flood back in the '30s floated people out through Arkansas and Mississippi. The Mississippi River overflowed. But I always found a way of doing something to help my mother. When I was twelve years old, I was out on Front Street with the poor children, and I could hear them singing in the auditorium. I didn't have a ticket. And do you know, I sang my way in there!

I started singing outside. That wind was cuttin', but I sang. They had a choir inside, and word was they'd give the poor children who sang in the choir a bag. The bag had a pair of jeans, a shirt, a sweater, and a couple of pairs of socks and a great big stocking with peppermint candy and fruit in it. The police stood there and listened to me sing. I didn't pay no attention. One of them went inside and got Ms. Lucie Campbell, and brought her outside. He asked, "What do you hear?" "I hear an angel singing," she said. And he said, "If you don't get him and take him in there, and let him get a bag, I'm gonna put ya in jail." "If you don't get him a ticket, I'm gonna have you fired," she said back.

He got the ticket. She took me in. I sang and this was the time to give the toys and gifts to the poor children. They gave me two bags, one for me and one for my brother, Van. Mr. Joe Brennan, who was president of the Memphis Power & Light Company, sent my mother two turns [loads] of coal. We lived in an alley there off of Main Street, down from the auditorium. Our next-door neighbors would wait till we'd go to sleep and help themselves. I'd say, "Mama, somebody's getting our coal." She'd say, "Go on to sleep, Robert; they're cold too."

EDWARD BROOKE

Born in Washington, D.C., on October 26, 1919

Former U.S. Senator from Massachusetts, attorney, consultant

After serving in Africa and in Italy as an officer in the Army during World War II, Edward Brooke began a long and distinguished career as an attorney and public official. In 1962 he became the first African American elected as attorney general of Massachusetts. He was also the only Massachusetts Republican to win a statewide election that year. As attorney general, he led the fight to uphold the constitutionality of the Voting Rights Act.

A black Republican Protestant in a state that was overwhelmingly white, Democratic, and Catholic, Brooke had persuaded voters to look beyond his race, party, and religion to his record. He explained to voters, "I'm trying to show that people can be elected on the basis of their qualifications and not their race."

Those qualifications served him well when he launched his campaign for the U.S. Senate in 1965. He beat then governor Endicott Peabody and became the first African American to serve in the Senate since 1881. During his tenure as senator, Brooke was a strong advocate for affirmative action, and minority business development, and helped achieve an increase in Medicare funding.

After leaving Congress in 1979, Brooke continued to work for the causes he supported while in office. He headed the National Low-Income Housing

Coalition, joined feminist Gloria Steinem in forming a pro-choice group called Voters for Choice, and appeared before his former colleagues to voice support for federal grants to help the poor purchase fuel oil.

In addition to his book, Challenge of Change: Crisis in Our Two-Party System, *his extensive writing on legal and political issues has appeared in both professional journals and news publications across the country. A recipient of the NAACP's Spingarn Award, Brooke has also received thirty-four honorary degrees.*

*P*olitics is the art of the possible. There are also lots of compromises. I've always wanted elective office as opposed to appointive office because I've always believed that's where the power is. It's your power; it's not someone else's power. If you are appointed by the president, be it the secretary of anything, if it is a cabinet position or head of any agency, you are an extension of the presidency. So you have to follow the philosophy and the decisions made by the president. I always wanted to be in the seat of power.

And I wanted to prove that whites would vote for blacks. Blacks should be in the seat of power, with their own power base.

People have asked me many times, "Was race a factor in your elections?" There are some whites who did not vote for me because I was black. But there are some whites who voted *for* me because I was black. I think they balanced out each other. The masses of people who voted for me believed I could do the job better than the candidate against whom I was running; that's what I honestly believe.

The reason I am Republican, first of all, is because in 1950 I won the Republican nomination [for state representative]. I did not win the Democratic nomination. In 1952, again, I won the Republican nomination, not the Democratic nomination. And I have a loyalty to the party. But even more importantly, in Massachusetts it was the Republican Party that had desegregated the National Guard. It was the party, I believe, that was much more progressive than the Democratic Party. The Democrats were supporting McCarthyism, for example. I was against McCarthyism. And the Republican Massachusetts Party was against McCarthyism. It was a moderate wing of the Republican Party. Republicans in Massachusetts are more moderate than conservative. Barry Goldwater, along the line, changed a lot of that.

I am a moderate to liberal Republican. On social issues I am a liberal. No one expected me not to be pro—civil rights or pro—women's rights or pro—civil liberties. On economic issues, I've always believed that a man or woman should do for themselves; the government should do only those things which men and women can't do for themselves. That was not a Goldwater statement; that was an Abraham Lincoln statement.

But I believe the party should have a heart as well as a head, and recognize that there are things that people *can't* do for themselves. And, therefore, government must do it for them. But I don't like huge government or a huge bureaucracy. I have a conservative bent in that regard. I believe in problem solving. I wanted to be a problem solver.

I've never isolated myself from black politicians. I believe most blacks in Congress are Democrats because they represent predominantly black districts. When I went to Washington, I was the only black in the Senate.

It was uncomfortable for the other black members of Congress as well as for me. I wasn't in the House. I was in the Congress, but not in the House. I was in the Senate. There was no other reason for my not being a member of the Black Caucus. I was not a part of it. I don't remember ever being officially invited to join the Black Caucus.

Had I been invited, I would've had to give it some thought—the Caucus was Democratic, always. Pure politics—forget the racial issue—we are talking pure politics now. It would not have worked well.

I knew when I went to the Senate that I was charting new ground, that what I did in the Senate would have an impact for all blacks in the future who either aspired to or got elected to the Senate. I knew I could not restrict my interests and my activities and use my energy only on black issues. I had to be interested in world issues, and certainly national issues. I had always believed all issues affected blacks as well as whites. You can't pass a bill in this country that doesn't affect all the people in some way. If you raise taxes, you raise taxes on blacks as well as whites; it's the same if you lower the taxes. If you defend against nuclear warfare, you are defending blacks as well as whites.

I didn't want to restrict my activities only to civil rights issues. Sometimes the black community didn't understand that because I made the statement once that I am not a civil rights leader, I am a politician who is black. I don't think there is anyone in the Congress now or before who has a better record on civil rights, but that doesn't mean I was there doing nothing but civil rights legislation.

Had I done that, it would've made it much more difficult for blacks to be elected in the future, and I wouldn't have stayed there for a second term. I served twelve years, and lost for the wrong reasons, but that's another story.

Clarence Mitchell, who was the lobbyist for the NAACP, never put pressure on me for anything. He spent his time between the House and the

Edward Brooke, Howard University, ca. 1940

Senate, but mostly in the Senate. His job was to get votes for civil rights legislation and to stop anti–civil rights legislation. Some of us called him the 101st United States senator. We discussed legislation frequently. When I judged the timing was right for me to take a very visible public leadership role on any issue, I did. There were times I felt the leadership should come from someone else, if that someone else was better able to achieve our goal.

Many things that black politicians and officeholders have achieved have gone unrecognized by the white press. I don't think many people in this country today know that I was a big fighter for the Japanese Americans and the legislation which gave remunerations [for World War II wrongs] and held hearings all over the country. They don't know that, or my role in the extension of the Voting Rights Act. There was never an issue like it that came before the Senate.

I first encountered the Voting Rights Act when I was attorney general of Massachusetts. During that time, the Voting Rights Act was passed in 1964. I got the former solicitor general Archibald Cox to agree to accept an appointment from me as his special assistant attorney general for the purpose of arguing the constitutionality of that act before the Supreme Court. I also got eighteen states to join as *amicus* in that case. And we won. I am very proud of that. When the Voting Rights Act came up for extension in the '70s, I was chief proponent for the extension in the Senate. If you read the congressional record, you will see that I had to stay up and battle for that. I was in the forefront of the leadership for any legislation involving civil rights on the Senate side.

I take great consolation knowing that the record is there, and that I did it not necessarily for credit. But every politician wants credit. Of course, on the other hand, I did it because I believed in it.

I would like to believe that if I were a white man, I would've done the same thing. You may say that's naive, but to me it isn't. I don't believe that black men or black women have a monopoly on this at all. I think there are white people out there who believe just as strongly as we black people believe in some of these issues. They are *human* issues.

I was in the position where something could be done about these human issues, because I was in the power structure. That's my argument: if you want to get it done, you've got to be where the power is. I watch black leaders and politicians around the country, hoping that they will come to the Senate.

I knew Martin Luther King Jr. in his early days, because he came to the Boston University School of Divinity. As a matter of fact, he was initiated into my fraternity, Alpha Phi Alpha. I knew him then, but lost track of him and watched and admired the work he was doing and the courage and the fearlessness that he demonstrated during the Civil Rights Movement. When I was in the Senate and he had come out against the Vietnam War, trying to discourage blacks from joining the armed forces, we met and I said to him, "Well, Martin, do you think your position on the war is going to impinge upon your effectiveness as a Civil Rights leader?" Without pausing he said, "Ed, I was a preacher of the Word of God long before I was a Civil Rights leader."

I got an invitation from Rap Brown during the Black Power Movement to meet with him and some of his associates in New York. My political staff advised me not to go. I said, "I'm not going to take that advice. I want to go. I want to meet with him. I want to hear what he has to say. I want to find out why he wants to meet with me." They said, "Why don't you invite him to the Senate?" I had suggested that, but he wanted me to come to them. It was a meeting on Seventh Avenue, down in the basement. When my car drove up Rap came out with one or two of his lieutenants and escorted me in. There were maybe thirteen people there, big Afros, arms folded, the whole bit. They pulled out a chair and set it in front of them so they would be looking at me and I would be looking at them, nobody on my side. Rap was sitting with the people.

They didn't say welcome, or anything of that nature, and before I said anything, he says, "You're not black." Boom. I just didn't respond. He said, "You're part of the establishment. You're what's wrong with America."

I said, "Do you mean by being a member of the United States Senate, that I'm wrong with America?" He said, "Just being there makes you one of them. You're not one of us." "It is important for one of us to be in a seat of power," I said. He said, "Oh, that's not power."

I said, "Well, that's where the money is, that's where all the programs are that affect not only your lives, but the lives of millions of people, black and white. That's where the Army is. That's where the Navy and Marine and the Air Corps are. That's where the missiles are. That's where the power is."

"Not for long," he said.

I said, "I deal with facts, and the fact is, you don't have that kind of power. And what black people need is to be in a position of power. You should be happy that I'm sitting in the United States Senate."

"What do you mean, I should be happy? We're not happy about that at all."

I asked, "Where would you have me?" He said, "Where would you want to be?" I said, "Exactly where I am." I wanted to be there because that is where I could do the most good.

I would say that I was there almost two hours. Nothing came of it. I don't think I persuaded them; obviously they weren't persuading me. I think they understood what I was saying, even though they wouldn't endorse what I was saying. They walked me out to the car, there was no "Thank you for coming," there was no smiling, there was no handshaking, any of that thing. I got in my car, rode out to LaGuardia, got a plane, came back to work.

I've said, particularly to young black children, your place is anywhere you want it to be. It's left up to you. You make that decision.

To young politicians, I want to make a plea for elective office. Seek power. There's nothing wrong with power if it's used wisely and used rightly. Power is essential. Power is what gets things going. It can be used for good as well as for evil.

JEROME BROOKS

Born in Port Arthur, Texas, on January 15, 1918

First African American real estate broker in the city of Port Arthur;

retired U.S. postal official

Selected and interviewed by

NVLP Fellow Ileana Simien, Praise View A&M

Over the course of his long career, Jerome Brooks served as superintendent of the U.S. Postal Service in Port Arthur, Texas, while simultaneously managing his own real estate company. In the 1960s, the U.S. Postal Service granted him a leave of absence to participate in an urban renewal project, for which Brooks served as the acquisitions officer in the purchasing of property for the construction of two new schools for African American children. Now retired, he continues to live in Port Arthur.

The best thing I can say to blacks coming up today is, "Don't worry about what color you are." I've had people all over the country say, "Jerome, why don't you go ahead and pass for white. Nobody'll ever know the difference. Your whole family's bright. You could do this and you could do that." I know a lot of white mulattos that's passing for white and don't have what I have. I did it my way. I said, "I'm going to get mine honestly, and I'm going to get it because I'm going to fight for it."

I was born in the back of Saint Mary's Hospital in Port Arthur on old Fourth Avenue over the laundry room. They had three beds in there for "colored"—I'm going to use the word because that's what they used back then.

[When I grew up] I worked on the wharf. Later on, I got a job working at the refinery. But after working out there about six months, an incident occurred. We were eating lunch. All of the adults knew me, saw me raised up in Port Arthur. A couple of them were related to me too.

Older men say things that they can't say in front of a younger person, so I would always go and sit a distance from them, where I wouldn't be in their way.

This particular Monday at lunch, the white boss-man asked one of the men who liked excitement, "What'd you do over the weekend—chase nigger women all over town, the west side?"

And he said, "No, man, I was trying to sell my eggs." He sold eggs for extra money.

And he asked another one, "What'd you do over the weekend, same thing, chase nigger women?"

And he went on down the line, and another one said, "No, I'm a married man. I don't do that. I don't go out and chase women or drink or nothing."

He finally got through with them. I was over there tending to my business. A shovel was turned upside down, and I was sitting on it. And he came over by me, and hollered out, "Red, what'd you do over the weekend; chase them nigger women, too, huh?"

"No, come to think about it, I didn't," I said. "I was on the east side chasing the white women." What'd I want to say that for!

He came over there and stood up over me and said, "Nigger, don't you know who you're talking to?"

"Yeah, I know who I'm talking to. Didn't you know who you were talking to when you asked me the question you did? I ain't never called you a cracker or a redneck. Why'd you call me a nigger?"

He kept saying, "Don't you ever do nothing like that again, nigger."

I said, "You say that one more time, I'm going to hit you over the head." I stood up. "One more time, and I'll hit you over the head with a shovel." He said it again, like a fool, and I hit him and knocked him out cold.

I didn't intend to kill him or nothing, I just wanted to let him know that some people didn't want to be called niggers.

He lied and told his boss that he wasn't bothering me, said he didn't know why I came over there—came over there!—and hit him. "Ask them niggers over there," he said.

They didn't say a word in my defense, not one word. The superintendent of the plant came out. He knew me when I was in high school. He said, "You're a damn liar, Bob. This boy's been working out here every summer for many years. I never had any trouble with him. This is the first time he's ever been involved in anything like this. He doesn't sit down around the older men, and he doesn't debate whether he wants to do something or not. If you tell him to do it, he'll do it, if he can do it."

"Well, you need to fire him," he said. "He hit me in the head for nothing."

"You know who needs to be fired? You." He said, "Jerome, go get in my car." And he took me to another supervisor's job.

This was 1936. The longshoremen were on strike, and the supervisor on the dock had scabs working. Scabs were nonmembers of the longshoremen's local. We [union members] couldn't go in the yard and work because we were on strike. They were hauling the nonmembers in there in boxcars. They stayed in there; they couldn't come out because if they came out, somebody would hurt them, beat them up.

My boss came over and said, "Brooks, you have to go on the dock, and [work] with the scabs over there."

I said, "Not on your life."

He said, "Why?"

I said, "My daddy's a longshoreman. You think I'm going to take the food out of my mouth working with scabs? No way."

He said, "Well, I tell you what. Either you go on the docks or you go on the highway."

I said, "Good-bye. Highway, here I come." And I left.

ROSCOE LEE BROWNE

Born in Woodbury, New Jersey, on May 2, 1922

Actor, director, writer

Roscoe Lee Browne is internationally renowned for his commanding presence on stage, screen, and television. He made his stage debut in the New York Shakespeare Festival production of Julius Caesar in 1956. His deeply resonating voice and impeccable diction won him numerous other roles on the Shakespearean stage in the 1960s, including his highly acclaimed portrayal of the Fool in the 1962 production of King Lear in New York's Central Park. Since then, he has appeared on and off Broadway, in theater festivals throughout the United States and abroad, as well as in film and on television.

Prior to beginning his acting career, Browne enjoyed international acclaim as a middle-distance runner. A member of ten Amateur Athletic Union teams, he was twice the American indoor champion in the 1000-yard run and, in Paris, ran the world's fastest 800 meters in 1951. Two weeks later, he set the American citizen record for the 1000 meters. During this time, he also worked as an instructor of French and comparative literature at his alma mater, Lincoln University, in Pennsylvania.

Considered by many to be the quintessential American character actor, Browne has appeared in more than thirty films, including Hamlet, The Mambo Kings, Black Like Me, Brother Minister: The Assassination of

Malcolm X, The Liberation of Lord Byron Jones, *and* The Cowboys; *he was the narrator of two Oscar-nominated films,* Babe *and* The Ra Expeditions. *For his work in theater, Browne has received 3 NAACP Image Awards, 3 LA Drama Critics Circle best actor awards, and a Helen Hayes Medallion. His numerous television appearances have consistently shown his versatility and commanding presence as an actor. He could inspire audiences with his acclaimed portrayal of Frederick Douglass, and laugh with them as part of the ensemble cast of the culturally groundbreaking comedy* Soap. *He won an Emmy Award for his appearance on* The Cosby Show *and received Emmy nominations for his guest appearances on* Barney Miller, Falcon Crest, *and* Spiderman *(animated version).*

In addition to acting, Browne is an accomplished poet and short story writer. Audiences have enjoyed works such as A Hand Is on the Gate, *a celebration of the African American experience in poetry and song, directed and created by Browne. The production eventually ran on Broadway and won two Tony Award nominations.*

Having contributed his substantial talents to many genres, Roscoe Lee Browne has established himself as one of the great artistic figures of the twentieth century.

*D*uring the Depression, my father, a minister, worked as a parcel post deliverer in Philadelphia, which is eleven miles away from our home. I have a sister who's a little bit older than I, three older brothers, and one younger. We were six. One of my brothers told me, at some point, that

The Browne family in 1933; Roscoe Lee at bottom left

we lived "up south." There was precious little racial friction in Woodbury, though. I know they say it's a city now, but we thought it was a little town.

I was aware of my father and other people going into what we called "Gun Town," an absolutely, unquestionably, almost ghettoized black section . . . to help some of the families, because men were out of work during the Depression.

There were more white children than there were black in my high school. I would not remember, on occasion, that I was black. In high school, I knew that I was going to go out for this play, and I'd forget: Roscoe, you're black and you're "up south," and you're not going to get it.

I had some difficulty with only two or three of the students. I may have been altogether objectionable, but I knew that their difficulty with me was that I had better grades in French than they did, and two of them had French nannies.

Many years later, I announced to three friends over dinner that tomorrow I'm going to become an actor. Mind you, I was already thirty-five years old. This was 1956. And one of them, Josephine Premice, said, "You're not a kid, you know."

Susan Fonda, who was then married to Henry Fonda, said, "You don't even know you're black," which really meant you don't know how tough it's going to be. And Leontyne Price said, "They'll have you bearing torches."

In about 1963 or '64, Joseph Papp [creator of the celebrated New York Shakespeare Festival, which brought free theatrical performances to the public in Central Park] asked me if I would direct an evening of love poetry [A Hand Is on the Gate], and I said sure. He picked a couple of actors and asked if I minded. I said no. He suggested all the right people. I mean, everybody was absolutely correct. I only had to bring in one that he hadn't thought of.

It was a marvelous thing to go digging through not only my memory, but all those books to find these great poets from slavery time to the present time. Langston Hughes not only came every day and every night to see it, but kept surprising us by bringing all of these living poets to the theater. He brought Margaret Walker, Gwendolyn Brooks, and Arna Bontemps. He just kept bringing them and bringing them.

It was such a good thing for the audience and for African Americans who had never heard any of these poets. It was an absolutely marvelously successful evening. Joseph said, "Does it shock you that even the police on horseback were stopping and listening to the poetry?" I said no. He said that he didn't think white Americans know anything about African American poetry. I said that a lot of African Americans don't know anything about African American poetry.

I don't think the struggle is over, or that it's a wide-open highway, but I think that more [African American actors] can get roles that we could not before; roles that are respectful, even. Although some of the stuff that's on television, I still regard that stuff—I shan't name any of it—as authentic crap.

Live in the present, but while [you're] living in the present, a very good, useful, loving, and great thing to do is to check out all of history, all of the past you can get hold of.

There is a lot of it. Some is gone; some of the past can't be found, but in the main it can be found. Checking that out, and living today, will really make the future easier for [young African Americans] as human beings, as a people.

Be critical thinkers. There's something to say for activism. It can sometimes tell you who you are. It can certainly tell you who you are not.

ELIZABETH CATLETT

Born in Washington, D.C., on April 15, 1919

Artist, educator

Acclaimed for her abstract sculptures, prints, and paintings, Elizabeth Catlett is one of the most prominent artists of the twentieth century. The celebration of strong black women and mothers is a consistent theme throughout her art, evident in such sculptures as her Homage to My Young Black Sisters *(1968) and various mother-child pairings.*

After becoming the first student to earn a master of fine arts degree in sculpture from the University of Iowa, in 1940, she exhibited her work in several group shows across the country. A turning point in her career occurred in 1946, when she accepted an invitation to work in Mexico City's Taller de Grafica Popular (TGP), a collective graphic arts and mural workshop.

In 1947 she produced her much celebrated I Am a Negro Woman *series of sculptures, prints, and paintings through a Julius Rosenwald Foundation fellowship. That same year, she married her second husband, Mexican painter Francisco "Pancho" Mora, with whom she had three sons, Francisco, Juan, and David.*

During the 1950s Catlett not only developed as an artist but also as a left-wing activist. As a result of her alliance with the TGP, then suspected of communist activities, she endured investigation by the House Un-American

Activities Committee during the height of the communist "witch hunts" led by Senator Joseph McCarthy. Her arrest as an undesirable alien by the U.S. government in 1959 and ongoing problems with the American embassy influenced her decision to become a Mexican citizen in the 1960s.

Making Mexico her home, she accepted in 1958 the position of professor of sculpture in the National School of Fine Arts at the Universidad Nacional Autonoma de Mexico. In the decades that followed, her artistic reputation grew. Catlett's tremendous contributions to the African American art movement have garnered her wide recognition even over the past decade. In February of 1998 the Neuberger Museum of Art at the State University of New York at Purchase honored Catlett with a fifty-year retrospective that traveled throughout the United States and Mexico. She was honored again in 2003, when the International Sculpture Center, the world's leading sculpture organization, granted her its Lifetime Achievement in Contemporary Sculpture Award.

Although retired from teaching, Catlett continues with her art. In 2003 she unveiled her monumental sculpture honoring the late author Ralph Ellison, who wrote the groundbreaking 1952 novel Invisible Man. *Commissioned by the City of New York Parks and Recreation Department, the monolithic work is situated in Riverside Park in Harlem.*

My mother was the daughter of ex-slaves. My father's mother was a slave. My father died before I was born. They had eight children, four boys and four girls, and they sent us through the highest education we could get. My mother came to Washington to help a relative with her dressmaking business and met my father. He had taught at Tuskegee with Booker T. Washington and Dr. [George Washington] Carver.

When my father died, my mother had already graduated from the Skosa Seminary, but she had a job scrubbing floors and hanging coats up in a club at night. People decided that was terrible. She had a cousin in Washington who was a surgeon and, I think, got her a job as a public school attendance officer.

We lived in Northwest Washington, where most of the African Americans who were in more or less medium circumstances lived. We didn't go into the white area except to shop or on special occasions like the Fourth of July, to see the fireworks at the Washington Monument, or to Rock Creek Park at Easter time.

I liked to draw and paint, and my mother used to bring me materials. She was very supportive. I would draw paper dolls when I was about eight or nine years old. My paper dolls had huge wardrobes. Friends would ask me sometimes, "Make me one. Make me one." We didn't have any money at all. I got the idea to charge them five cents for a doll and an outfit. When I went to high school, I used to do drawings, projects for the teachers. I *really* got paid for those!

When I was in high school, I didn't know that there were very few black women artists. But I decided that is what I wanted to do, to be an artist. I didn't know much about art schools and decided to go to the Carnegie Institute of Technology in Pittsburgh, because I had cousins living there. When I got to Carnegie Tech, they told me that they didn't have any Negroes. People said, "You're not going to get in there."

I spent two weeks at Carnegie Tech taking competitive exams working with different materials. We had assignments and would work on them at

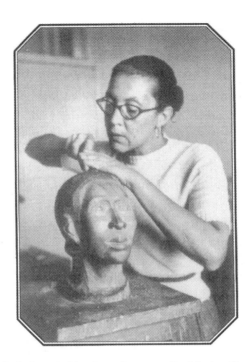

Elizabeth Catlett working in sculpture studio, Mexico City, ca. 1947

night. In class the teacher would hold up our work and ask, "Who likes this?" People always said they liked what I was doing. One day I was going up the steps to my locker and heard a teacher say, "It's too bad that she's colored." I thought that he meant that I was going to have problems with my career. But what he meant was that I wasn't going to get in to the program. When I got a letter saying that I wasn't admitted, I was very surprised and very angry. I went back home and my mother said, "Well, you can go to Howard University." And that is what I did.

This is the advice that I would give: try and do something constructive, not to be rich and not to be famous, not to be important or not to have five wives—notice I said five *wives,* I didn't say five husbands. Make your life important. Give of yourself. It's not easy. Think about other people. Base what you are doing on something that has to do with all of us. That is what gave me direction in art. When I decided that I was going to work with the problems of black women, I wanted to make people see them as beautiful, dignified, strong people, instead of, as Ralph Ellison says, invisible. A lot of artists say they work to do their own work, and if people like it, all right, if they don't like it, all right. I work to see what people think about what I'm doing.

My husband didn't like Jacob Lawrence's painting when he saw reproductions. We went one night to an exhibit for him at the Brooklyn Museum. It was full of black people and Jake's paintings. Pancho, my husband [also an artist], looked at them and said, "I have to tell Jake how I feel." He went over and said to Jake, "I never liked your work when I saw reproductions. But I'm seeing it now with this roomful of black people, and it looks like these people are looking back at the people in your paintings, and the people in your paintings are looking back at them." I thought, "That's what an artist wants."

RAY CHARLES

Born in Albany, Georgia, on September 23, 1930

Singer, musician, composer

—◆—

Ray Charles is one of the most influential figures in contemporary music. As Tom Piazza, author of Blues Up and Down: Jazz in Our Time, *observes, "No other American musician since World War II, or before it for that matter, has performed with such artistic and commercial success in as many apparently disparate genres. He has played and sung rhythm-and-blues, soul, country, jazz, pop, and rock; somehow he has found a way to be absolutely himself in each one."*

Born in Albany, Georgia, in 1930, Charles moved to Greenville, Florida, as a child, where he was raised in extreme poverty. Charles contracted glaucoma at age five, lost his sight completely by age seven, and lost his mother soon thereafter. In spite of such hardships, Charles learned to read and write music in Braille and became proficient on several musical instruments by the time he left the St. Augustine School for the Deaf and Blind. Charles later told Jet *magazine that his mother reminded him, "You might not be able to do things like a person who can see. But there are always two ways to do everything. You've just got to find the other way."*

Ray Charles indeed found a way, and has become a living legend. Countless organizations have paid tribute to his creative genius with their highest honors. He has received twelve Grammy Awards, including the prestigious Lifetime Achievement Award. He also serves as honorary lifetime chairman of the Songwriters Hall of Fame. Throughout his career, Charles has been credited with influencing many other musicians, including Otis Redding, Stevie Wonder, James Brown, Steve Winwood, and Joe Cocker.

Many of his songs have become musical-cultural touchstones. His classic rendering of "Georgia on My Mind" was officially named Georgia's state song in 1979. In 2003 the Library of Congress selected his long-standing hit "What'd I Say" as one of the fifty historic recordings to be preserved in the new National Recording Registry.

His pioneering approach to music has created an enduring and eclectic style. As he wrote in his autobiography, Brother Ray, *"Music is nothing separate from me. It* is *me."*

My mom had to leave school to work in the fields when she got to about the fourth or fifth grade, and my dad didn't finish school either. He went to work for the railroad, so we were very poor. To give you an idea of the way it was in the community, sometimes if my mom needed some flour, she'd borrow it from the lady next door. If the lady next door needed some sugar, she'd borrow it from my mom. That's how we were able to survive. We all had gardens and raised our food.

I don't know where she got this inner sense, but somehow my mother went against everything that was supposed to happen with a blind kid in a little town. The neighbors all thought she was too brutal toward me, too cruel,

Ray Charles, publicity photo, 1960

because my mom made me cut wood and wash clothes, even build a fire under the pot where you boiled the clothes. People thought that was abusive.

Mom had the attitude, "He's got to learn, and just because he's blind, he's not stupid. He can find ways. He may not do it the way I do it, but he can find a way to do it for himself. He has to learn how to be independent." She always preached this to me. She'd tell me, "Even friends who love you, they're not going to have time for you all the time. They got their lives, and you got to learn how to do things for yourself. You are not going to carry a cup, period."

Of course, in those days, that's what most blind people did. They stood around; they had a cup. Some of them could play a little guitar or something, and that was the way they made it. I don't know where she got this gumption from.

The first time I saw my mom cry was when the people in church got up and criticized her for making me cut wood. "A chip could fly up and hit that boy," they were saying. She stood up crying, could hardly speak, and said, "Of course a chip can fly up and hit him. But I can see, and a chip can fly up and hit me." That's the kind of woman she was. She'd say, "Now look, I want you to learn how to get around by yourself without seeing. And the way we are going to do this is, I'm going to place some chairs in certain areas of this room. And I want you to learn how to navigate these chairs. I want you to learn how, when you go into a place, to observe what it's like."

No dog and no cane. You know I'm going to walk into things, but it taught me to remember where things were. I do that until this day. When I go into hotels, I survey the room and then after I do that, I remember where everything is. That way I don't walk into anything, I don't bump into a wall. When people see me get around, they say, "Oh, I know he can see something; now, come on! Did you see how he walked past that thing like that?" They just can't envision that I truly can't see.

[I got my first piano from] Riley Pitman, a great boogie-woogie pianist. Any time he started playing that piano, I don't care what my buddies were doing at the time, I would immediately stop. That music just stopped me in my tracks. I'd run in there and jump up on the little stool, and start hitting the keys with all my fingers.

What's marvelous about this man is that he could have said, "Hey, kid, don't you see I'm practicing? Get away, go out there and play." But he didn't do that. He said, "Oh, you love music so much, but you don't hit the keys with your fist. I'm going to show you how to play a little melody with one finger." I was fascinated just to mash a key and get a sound. And then he showed me how to play, "Come out, little playmate, come. Boom, boom, boom, boom, boom." A little simple thing like that!

I love him until this day because had it not been for him, I don't think I would be what I am today. I'm very grateful to him, Lord rest his soul.

The best advice I can give young artists is have faith in yourself. I was lucky; I had free rein in the record companies I was with. None of them told me what to do, or how to do it, or when to do it. Unfortunately for the young artists that come up now, they got producers who tell them what to say, how to say it. When I listen to a lot of this stuff I hear today, so many of these kids sound so much the same. You had identity when I was coming up. If Ella Fitzgerald opened her mouth to sing one word, you knew that was Ella Fitzgerald. You knew that was Nat Cole. You knew that that was Frank Sinatra, or Barbra [Streisand].

But today—and I know I hear good, I know I do—record companies want you to sound like whoever had the last hit. Producers oppose artists who say, "Hey, I'm creating my stuff, I'm gonna do it the way I feel it, and you worry about the selling of it." You can't do that nowadays. It just doesn't work that way.

To young artists coming up, if you have faith in yourself, if you know what you're doing is good, keep on keeping on. And you know that you're good when you compare it with what you hear out there. Is your sound unique? If you believe in yourself, don't let anybody discourage you.

And above all, practice. I know that's a dirty word, but every great musician I know practices. Kids have so many diversions nowadays: they go to ball games; they've got this computer, that new electronic toy they sit at all day long. I'm not saying not to do these things, but allocate at least one hour a day to do nothing but practice for yourself.

MARY ALICE CHINEWORTH

Born in Rock Island, Illinois, on July 16, 1917

Member and former director of the Oblate Sisters of Providence,

the nation's first order of black nuns

———◆———

As a lifelong educator, activist, and seasoned leader of the country's first order of black nuns, Sister Mary Alice Chineworth has played a major role in developing the minds and spirits of countless black children. Inspired by her kindergarten teacher at age four, she felt the call to religious life. Much to her surprise, when she had grown old enough to express a formal interest in joining her teacher's religious order, she was rejected because she was black. She would be rejected once more before discovering and subsequently joining the Oblate Sisters of Providence in Baltimore.

These early setbacks did not stop Sister Mary Alice from moving forward to accomplish her goals. She spent some thirty years as a teacher, working primarily with children from Baltimore's African American community. Her leadership talents moved her increasingly toward administrative work, culminating in her appointment as president of Mount Providence Junior College. In 1970 Sister Mary Alice earned a doctorate in higher education from Catholic University in Washington, D.C. Beginning in 1973 she held several high-level positions within the Order of the Oblate Sisters of Providence, finally attaining the rank of superior general in 1989. She has been consistently outspoken in urging the Church to welcome more actively the advancement of African Americans and women.

Like many other religious orders, the Oblate Sisters of Providence are struggling to attract young people to their ranks. Still, Sister Mary Alice perseveres, "As long as there are poor children—disadvantaged, marginalized children—to educate, we will be there."

Everybody in [my high] school knew that I was going be a Sister of Charity of the Blessed Virgin Mary. Those of us who wanted to enter the convent talked about it freely. One time when I was a junior, Sister said to me, "Have you given up the idea of being a Sister?" I said, "Oh, no." She said, "Well, what order are you entering?" I said, "What order? I didn't know there *were* other orders. Yours is the only order I know." She began to cry and said, "You can't come to us because you're colored. But here are the names of three black orders."

She gave me the names of the Sisters in Harlem, the Sisters in New Orleans, and the Sisters of Providence in Baltimore. I wrote identical letters to the three and sat back and waited for God to show me what to do. I said, "This is in His hands." I got the first [acceptance] letter from the Harlem Sisters. The second was from New Orleans, but I said, "I don't want to go there." My parents always avoided the South because of racism. Not realizing that Baltimore was southern too, I said, "I like that better." I liked everything they said about it. They were the first of the black orders, founded over a hundred years ago, and it just sounded right to me.

So I responded affirmatively to them, and [we] began to correspond.

Mary Alice Chineworth, high school portrait

Nowadays they fly back and forth to visit, but in those days you did everything by letter, not even by phone.

I got a letter of acceptance. My father took me on the train, but we saw very little of [Baltimore]. I saw the station, and I saw the convent.

There is one thing that might shock people. The Sisters begged; we literally begged every Friday. Two of us [from the convent] went to the fish market, and each of us had a market basket. We would go through the stalls, and they would throw fish into the basket. When the baskets were filled, we took a cab home, and we had fresh fish for dinner on Friday. Those were the days when you didn't eat meat on Friday.

But every day two of us were told to go to the bakery up the street, where they would give us day-old bread. We were a very poor order, always have been. And I suppose we always will be.

One of the surprises of my life was when the superior general [of the convent] said to me, "What would your friends think of you now?" I was dressed in this habit to go out to the fish market. I imagined fish markets as beautiful and sanitary, that we would pick out the fish we needed and wanted. So the reality was a blow. But I loved it. I loved everything about the life. I never had an unhappy day in it.

I was just born for it. There are calls like that, and they're blessings. Some people struggle with the call, but I never did struggle. I never got homesick and wanted to go back home or anything like that. I have been very fortunate in being permitted by the order to do things that were self-fulfilling.

Black women, more than any other group of people, look upon us wonderingly. They wonder if we're for real. They wonder about our sex lives. They can't believe we don't have money; that our allowance is $40 a month and we make do with that. That's part of our poverty vow.

We get the most skepticism when a nun is well dressed. Many orders have come out of the habit. [Some women] think, "Why be a nun? I'm a career woman and I can do everything that you do." The community life is the difference. Community life is what separates the two, the career woman and the religious woman.

Community life is difficult, extremely difficult. It's very different from communal living. It's difficult because of personalities, all these women living together. Some like it hot, and some like it cold; some like the window up, some like it down. There is always somebody who rubs you the wrong way, but in Christian charity, you love everyone, and you really do sincerely love them. They become closer than your own blood sisters, but you could just kill them. You never get away from it; that's why so many sisters have opted to live alone. Hopefully, as you grow older, you get more tolerant.

It's very important to see one of your own in leadership positions in the black community. It's important to children to see what they can become. I've known some very wonderful pastors who are white, and who've done a wonderful job, but I wish that there were enough priests of color, African American priests, to serve.

As Sisters, if you get any five of us together, we're either from five different states or five different countries. We've always taken in Caribbean people. We have Cubans; we have Puerto Ricans, Costa Ricans, Hondurans, Belizeans—we have them all. There are cultural differences, but we have learned to live as an intercultural group very well.

Women priests would add a wonderful dimension to the Catholic faith. The early church in the time of Christ had a lot of women, and you read about them in the Bible. We know that the apostles were married, and I'm sure wives helped their husbands who became the first bishops of the church.

In the time before celibacy was imposed upon priests, all kinds of happy things were happening [including] married clergy and their families. I fail to see anything in the Bible that would prohibit it, but there's an ideology at play here and a deep-seated prejudice against women priests in the Catholic Church.

A leader is one who energizes people to go forward toward a goal that's very important to the whole group, who has a vision and is willing to sacrifice and move toward it, even if it means suffering and death. We have women who are ministering to people all over the place, but [women priests] can't hear [these people's] confessions sacramentally.

Having women priests would be a great gift to the church.

In time, it will come.

SHIRLEY CHISHOLM

Born in Brooklyn, New York, November 30, 1924

Former U.S. Congresswoman, educator, author

Shirley Anita St. Hill Chisholm was the first African American woman elected to the United States Congress, where she served as the representative for the Twelfth District of New York from 1969 until 1982. In 1972 she was the first black woman from a major party to actively run for the presidency of the United States.

Raised and educated in Barbados and the Bedford-Stuyvesant area of Brooklyn, New York, Chisholm trained to be a teacher at Brooklyn College. She learned the arts of organizing and fund-raising from her experience in the Delta Sigma Theta sorority and the National Association for the Advancement of Colored People.

During her teaching career, Chisholm developed a keen interest in politics. In 1964 she was elected to the New York State Assembly and then in 1968 successfully ran for the U.S. Congress.

Always considering herself to be a political maverick, Chisholm protested against defense budget expenses while social programs suffered. She supported pro-choice legislation. She argued that women be admitted to male-dominated professions — particularly black women, who had been shunted into stereotypical maid and nanny roles. Her antiwar and women's liberation views made her a popular figure among college students.

Civil rights for blacks, women, and the poor, reforms in the U.S. judicial system and in prisons, police brutality, gun control, tolerance of political dissent, and new approaches to drug abuse prevention and treatment were issues she consistently spoke out on when she ran for the presidency. George McGovern won the Democratic presidential nomination, but Chisholm captured 10 percent of the delegates' votes. As a result of her candidacy, Chisholm made Gallup's list of the ten most admired women in the world.

After her campaign, Chisholm continued to serve in the U.S. House of Representatives for another decade. As a member of the Black Caucus, she saw black representation grow in Congress, and welcomed other black women as U.S. representatives.

Chisholm cofounded the National Political Congress of Black Women in 1984 and worked vigorously for Reverend Jesse Jackson's presidential campaigns in 1984 and 1988. She also served as Purington Professor at Mount Holyoke College, in Massachusetts, where she taught politics and women's studies. In 1985 she was a visiting scholar at Spelman College before retiring from teaching in 1987.

My grandmother would always check my homework. Each night she would say, "Repeat [your homework assignment] to me," and if I didn't stand up straight, she said, "Child, you got to stand up straight, let the world see you coming." That's why I'm so erect!

Two other women influenced me a great deal.

Mary McLeod Bethune said to me, "You're smart; you're a very smart girl, but you must stand and fight." I'll never forget her words. "You must fight; you must fight."

Eleanor Roosevelt came to New York City when I was in a debating contest for the whole city of New York, and I won! I'll never forget this tall woman, her hair in a chignon, wearing this little porkpie hat. She was very ugly, but the moment she opened her mouth, you felt a warmth. It was beautiful. She said to me, "Shirley St. Hill, you're very smart, you're intelligent; you must fight, you must get up and don't let anybody stand in your way; even a woman can do it."

[My experience in the Ninety-seventh U.S. Congress] was one of the most difficult of my life. For the first two to three months, I was miserable. The gentlemen did not pay me any mind at all. When I would go to the lunchroom to eat, they would not sit at the same table with me.

It was horrible. Two little incidents will show what it was like for me. I had to have a sense of humor about a lot of things.

I did not know that in the little dining room beneath the House the tables were designated to state delegations—a table for New York, a table for Alabama. [One day] I sat at an empty table and ordered my lunch. I was very hungry that day, and I got a little bit of everything, plus dessert and salad. I always took *The New York Times* and read it while I was eating, because nobody would sit by me.

I felt something hovering above me. I looked up and if looks could kill, I would have been dead. I was seated at the Georgia delegation table.

"You're sitting at the wrong table," the glaring man said.

I said, "What did you say?"

He said, "I says, you're sitting at the wrong table."

"What table is this?"

"Georgia delegation."

"Oh," I said, "but, you see, the tables do not have any labels. I didn't know. Tomorrow I will find out where New York sits and eat there." I continued to eat.

"I says," he continued, "you're sitting at the Georgia delegation table. If you don't move from here, I will so and so and so." I began to feel sorry for him; he was hungry. I decided to use a different psychological approach. I said, "You're hungry, aren't you?" For the first time he gave me a smile. I repeated, "You're hungry."

"Sure, I'm hungry."

"I know what your problem is. Your problem is you're hungry and you cannot sit at this table because a black person is seated at the table. Isn't that right?"

"Yeah."

"I am going to help you. You see that table over there?" There was a table diagonally across from where I was sitting. "And there's nobody at it. Look, you go over and you sit at that table, order your lunch, and if anybody bothers you, you tell 'em to see Shirley Chisholm." I thought this would embarrass this Georgia congressman, but it did not. He went right over to the table, and sat down!

Another gentleman sat on the aisle seat on the House floor. My office was on the other side of the building, so when I came to the floor he could see me coming. I would sit right behind him.

And every day as I approached he would cough badly. One day I said to Brock Adams, representative from the state of Washington, "Why doesn't somebody do something for that poor man. He sounds like he has TB. There's something wrong with him."

Shirley Chisholm, congresswoman from New York, age 30

He said, "Shirley, I was waiting for you. I want to tell you something. You've got to do something. Every time he sees you coming through, he starts coughing, and then when you come by his seat, he gets his handkerchief out, he spits in the handkerchief, in your face."

This was his way of greeting me in the United States House of Representatives.

"He does, Brock?" I said.

"Uh-huh. What are you going to do about it?"

I said, "Watch me tomorrow." I had a sweater suit, and the jacket had big pockets. I purchased a male handkerchief and put it in the pocket, and the next day, when I came in, sure enough, he started coughing. I said to myself, "Uh-huh. Baby, I'm going to fix you today."

When he pulled the handkerchief out to meet my face and then spit in the handkerchief, I pulled a handkerchief out just in time to spit in it and throw it in his face. "Beat you to it today," I said to him.

From that day, he never coughed anymore.

The men upstairs in the balcony, including the newspaper men, saw this and almost toppled over the top. They roared. The Speaker had to say, "There'll be order in this House." I had allies. People were roaring, "Shirley, give it to him, give it to him." The House could be so boring at [other] times.

I had gone to the Congress as the first black woman, and I was invited for speaking engagements throughout the country. Everywhere people were encouraging me: "Ms. Chisholm, you should run." "You should run because you're a woman." "We never had a woman politician." "You're black." "We never had a black person run for president." "You speak Spanish." "You have a knowledge of the issues. Run." And that's what motivated me, spurred me on.

But the moment the announcement was made that I was going to make a bid for the presidency, all hell broke loose. All hell broke loose, from black men, white men, Puerto Rican men.

I looked neither to the south nor to the north, to the west nor to the east. Whatever I do, even today, I look only to God and my conscience for approval, not man. That's my motto. You go crazy if you look to man. Follow the dictates of your conscience. Do what you think and feel has to be done, and you'll be able to succeed.

I want history to remember me not just as the first black woman to be elected to Congress, not as the first black woman to have made a bid for the presidency of the United States, but as a black woman who lived in the twentieth century and dared to be herself. I want to be remembered as a catalyst for change in America.

ROBERT CHURCHWELL

Born in Clifton, Tennessee, on September 9, 1917

Retired journalist

Selected and interviewed by
NVLP Fellow Jerrad Davis, Fisk University

———————

Robert Churchwell was the first African American journalist to join the staff of the daily newspaper the Nashville Banner, *where he worked for thirty-one years. A graduate of Fisk University, Mr. Churchwell also served in the Army during World War II. He is a charter member of the National Association of Black Journalists.*

In 1950 I was unemployed. I had finished college and was a writer. One day the phone rang next door. We didn't have a phone, and my neighbor said, "You're wanted on the telephone." The man calling me was named Coyness Ennix. He was a lawyer and president of the Solid Block Organization, a civic group to get the vote out among Negroes. He was the leading Negro political leader in Nashville at the time, and the *Nashville Banner* had called him. They asked him to find a Negro to join their paper full-time. So they called me to come down and talk to them about a job with the *Banner.*

Well, I decided before I even went down there that I didn't want to work for the *Nashville Banner.* See, these were the early days of busing and desegregation. People attacked the government for even thinking about breaking down segregation. They would call us "niggers" on the floors of Congress. And the *Banner* would print that stuff. The *Banner* had a story one day on the front page about a Vanderbilt professor who said, "Research has shown that Negroes are direct descendants of apes and monkeys."

"No, I don't want to work for a paper like that," I said.

It was February, it was cold, and I was broke. I walked downtown to Ennix's office, and [the civic group members] told me what they wanted. They said, "This would be the first time a Negro worked full-time for a daily white newspaper in the South." So I said, "I'll think about it."

I walked back home. Ennix followed me and said the paper wanted to talk to me. He took me down to the *Banner.* Charles Moss, the executive editor, was interviewing me, and I wasn't there but fifteen minutes when he said he'd hire me. He didn't look at a thing I had written. I had written all those columns for the *Commentator.* I had written letters to the editor for the *Tennessean.* At that time the *Tennessean* paid you a dollar. I got a lot of dollars from the *Tennessean.* I needed them dollars.

Moss said that he would pay me $35 a week. He wanted me to start on Thursday or Friday of that week. That $35 loomed in my head, and I decided okay. He called and I said, "Okay. I'll go along with it, I'll take it, I'll take the job."

I go back down there, and the man said, "I want you to write Negro news. You write progressive Negro news, showing how Negroes are doing well in the Negro community." They had been publishing a page in the paper called "Happenings among Colored People." It was a slippage; you took the page out of the papers that went to the white community. Every Wednesday they ran that page.

Negroes knew they were taking that page out, and they'd stopped taking the *Banner* in droves. So they were desperate at the *Banner*. They were going to hire a Negro. They hired me so the *Banner* could start running pictures of Negroes and Negro stories all over the paper, not only in one part; not only in one place in the paper, but all over the paper.

I worked like a dog.

After he told me what he wanted me to do, he didn't give me a desk in the city room or in the newsroom. The first five years I had to write my stuff at home, in my front room.

I couldn't type. I didn't own a typewriter. Another church member, Mrs. Drake, who had taught me English at Pearl High, had a typewriter. She loaned me her typewriter.

I would get up in the morning at three and handwrite my news of the previous day, which was to go out all over the city. I printed it longhand, and my sister would type it for me.

After a while I decided, I'm going to buy me a typewriter. I bought a new portable Remington Rand typewriter and just began pecking my stuff out. I had to have it in by eight every morning to meet the first edition, which came out about eleven. The *Banner* had three editions a day, including a redline edition late in the evening, which carried the numbers for the numbers racket.

So the first five years I wrote my stuff at home, getting up at three every morning and walking from my home to [the *Banner* office] to give it to

Moss. Moss would give it to the city editor after he read it. That went on for five years.

I was covering the Negro community—the Boy Scouts, the Girl Scouts, YWCA, YMCA, Fisk, Tennessee State, churches, all churches, all black denominations. We're big on the Sunday churches. I worked every day of the week.

The *Banner* came out Monday, Tuesday, Wednesday, Thursday, and Friday, but I had to work on Sundays. That was my biggest day. After folks got used to me, they wanted to see their names in the paper, with pictures. I was always taking pictures.

In my work for the *Banner* for thirty-one years, I had my own civil rights experience—in the *Banner* newsroom. I called it "civil wrongs." They made me a news writer, then education writer, and [then] they gave me a desk in the newsroom. I'd moved up a little, I guess. But there I was, I'm the only Negro in the newsroom, with white women reporters, white men reporters. Only two women and about three of the men were friendly. Understand, this was in the fifties. I'm a Negro among these white folks, white reporters, and I can't count a half a dozen who were friendly, who would speak to me.

I didn't care about that. It didn't bother me if they didn't talk to me. I was there to do my work, and I did my work. If they wanted to talk, I would talk. If they wanted to be friendly, I'd be friendly.

You talk about civil rights. I call it civil wrongs. But my career was good. It was a test, being the first Negro under those conditions in journalism, and I had thirty-one years of success.

FLORA DAVIS CRITTENDEN

Born in Brooklyn, New York, on August 10, 1924

Member of the Virginia House of Delegates, former educator

Selected and interviewed by

NVLP Fellow Chikara Kennedy, Georgetown University

———◆———

After retiring from the Newport News Public School System in Newport News, Virginia, Flora Crittenden served one term on the Newport News City Council. At the encouragement of her former students and colleagues, she ran and was elected to the Virginia House of Delegates, where she has served since 1993. She is also an active member of Trinity Baptist Church, where she established a latchkey program that serves thirty children.

*B*oth of [my] parents are natives of Newport News, Virginia, and they moved to New York during the Depression to find work.

When I went to high school in 1939, I moved to Newport News, Virginia, and never went back to Brooklyn, although my parents were there. I moved here with my grandmother and my aunts. I really enjoyed high school. Newport News was quite different than New York. People believe that there was so much prejudice in the South, and it [wasn't as prevalent] in New York and other northern cities. That's not the case. I went to integrated schools before coming to Newport News. So often in the classroom setting, I was just ignored. And when they gave awards for citizenship and academics, I was never included. And I tried very hard to be a good student, and to be a model citizen, but I was never recognized.

That changed in high school [which was segregated]. I could belong to clubs and organizations. And I had teachers who cared, who really believed in us and pushed us to do our very best.

People talk frequently about our youth being our future, and how we need to show them the way. It's true. As a teacher, I felt if you gave young people the love and attention and guidance they need while they are young, you don't have to worry about the future. They will be prepared to take their places in society in the future. Young people are precious and interesting, like gems. They come in all different sizes, abilities, and attitudes. You've got to polish these gems to make them shine, for their true potential to emerge. In working with children, I believed very strongly in educating the whole child. Education involves more than academics; it involves helping [children] develop socially, physically, and emotionally. In planning for the education of young people, I took all of that into consideration and had objectives to help them grow in each of those areas.

Education is the key to all the doors, whether it's becoming a professional, getting a good job, making a livelihood for the family, or working with others. It's even the key to peace in the world. We have our problems because we don't understand one another, and we don't really *try* to understand one another. We need to make a real effort to come together as human beings and respect one another and accept that everybody has something to contribute, and that we might have different ways of doing it. We need to find peaceful solutions to living together, because if not, we're going to destroy ourselves.

That's all part of becoming an educated person. Today the emphasis is totally on academics. I think it's wrong. It's not just academics. We have to feel good about ourselves. Today people don't talk about self-image or understanding self as a means of understanding others and getting along with others. They see no point in that in the education system. It's all academic standards; testing to be sure that students have gained a body of information. Standards are fine, and we should have standards, but not to the omission of other important things.

I'm really opposed not to the standards but to allocating no time in the school day to help young people grow in areas other than academics. Not everybody goes to college. We have to interest students in many things. If we don't give them an opportunity to learn vocational and technical skills, and prepare them for the jobs that are in the world of work, then they have problems finding jobs when they leave school.

I'm very concerned about where we're headed today. Do we teach our children about the dangers of drugs? Do we teach our children how they can get caught up into that kind of lifestyle? Do we teach young people how to avoid pregnancy? No, we don't.

We establish laws that prevent young women from having abortions, based on talk about the sanctity of life. But after the children are born, is society concerned then about the sanctity of life? How these young people are going to grow and develop, whether or not they'll have the kind of environment they need, whether they'll get the proper care? No, we don't emphasize these things.

And those are the things that we need to emphasize.

We need to educate, educate, educate. Not just children but adults as well. Look at the illiteracy we have in our communities. And what are we doing on governmental levels? Cutting the funding to educate adults. And it's so important to our children to have parents who are literate, parents who can read with understanding, parents who can pass on helpful information to their children, parents who understand what's going on in the school system and can help their young people progress through the system.

Education is really what will make us free. Free to enjoy all the wonderful things we have around us—the joy of reading poetry, the joy of going to the beach and walking in the sand and listening to the motion of the waves, the joy of looking at the trees and watching the stars at night. It's emotionally uplifting when we can enjoy God's creations. Education is more than academic knowledge.

When I retired from the Newport News Public School System, I was fifty-six years old. After working in education, I was elected to the Newport News City Council. I was on for one term. My students first approached me about running for that seat, and I thought they were nuts.

"Uh-uh, not me. I'm not running for a political position!" I said, and rejected the whole notion. Howard Gwynn, who is the commonwealth's attorney in Newport News and one of my husband's former students, came to talk to me. He said, "Mrs. Crittenden, I understand you refused to run for city council."

"Yes."

"Well, why?"

"I am too old," I said, and gave all kind of excuses.

He looked me right in the eye. "I can't believe you are saying that. They're nothing but excuses," he said. "You always taught us we could do anything that we wanted to do if we worked at it. Why don't you use your own philosophy?"

It was a little bit embarrassing. I said, "Howard, I'll think it over and if I decide I'm going to run, you'll be the first one to know." And after thinking for a while, I decided I would run. And I did call Howard before I made the announcement.

That's how I got involved in politics. After my four-year term on the city council, I lost my bid for reelection. For a couple of years, I was just working in the community, but not in the political field per se. When the seat came up in the Virginia House of Delegates, my kids began saying, "Why don't you run?" So I did. I've been there now for eleven years.

My job is extremely frustrating. The philosophy of the legislature now is people need to pull themselves up by their bootstraps, they need to work for a living, secure their own needs, that there's no need for the kind of government help they've received in the past. Yes, people do need to work, and I go along with welfare reform, but if you're going to require people to work— back to education—we have to allow them to get the kind of education and training that will make them suitable for jobs that are going to pay decent salaries.

I feel like I have made a difference in some areas. It's very rewarding to get to know people from all walks of life. It is also rewarding when you feel that you have done something that makes a difference in the lives of people not just from your district but from all over Virginia.

RUBY DEE AND OSSIE DAVIS

Ruby Dee, born in Cleveland, Ohio, on October 27, 1924

Actress, civil rights activist, writer

Ossie Davis, born in Cogdell, Georgia, on December 18, 1917

Actor, civil rights activist, screenwriter, director

———

Ruby Dee's illustrious career has spanned more than five decades. As an actress she performed with the American Negro Theater and was the first black woman to play major roles in the prestigious American Shakespeare Festival. She went on to star in a range of socially conscious films, from A Raisin in the Sun *to* The Jackie Robinson Story *to* Just Cause *and* Do the Right Thing. *An Emmy Award–winner for her work in* Decoration Day, *Dee also received the Literary Guild Award in recognition of her plays, poems, and children's stories. A proud member of the NAACP, she has been inducted into both the Black Filmmakers Hall of Fame and the Theater Hall of Fame. Having worked on more than thirty collaborative projects with husband Ossie Davis, including her recent book and play* My One Good Nerve, *Dee's marriage remains more than fifty years strong, and they have 3 children.*

Actor, civil rights activist, screenwriter, director — Ossie Davis is a passionate man with many achievements. As an actor onstage and in films, he often starred in works focused on racial issues, including A Raisin in the Sun, No Way Out, *and* The Joe Louis Story. *He received an NAACP Image Award for his work in* Do the Right Thing. *He has appeared on several television series, such as* Queen, The Stand, *and* Evening Shade. *Davis was honored in 1984 with the Silver Circle Award by the Academy of Television Arts and Sciences. He wrote his first highly successful play,* Purlie Victorious, *and proceeded to direct productions like* Cotton Comes to Harlem *and* Black Girl. *For their more than fifty years of collaborative projects, Ossie Davis and Ruby Dee received the Presidential Medal for Lifetime Achievement in the Arts.*

Ms. DEE: I was never going to be a starlet at MGM because there was no such thing as black starlets in the stables of the big companies. Once that really hit me, I felt that devastation and sinking in my heart, and the longing. After that, a survival link kicked in, thank God. I made up my mind that there was going to be a way. I was encouraged by my stepmother, Emma, by my family, and people in school who selected me to read this and read that and to express myself and to write.

These people around me had lived through what I was just beginning to experience. I began to focus on all those things I could do, and I found such an excitement in being who I was as a human being, as a black girl in Harlem, which was an exciting and very supportive place to grow up. So another kind of thing supplanted all of the envy and all of the things that I thought I was missing. My life got filled with the possibilities, and filled with the challenges to make those possibilities become real.

How we touch each other, the people in our lives! I think of all the older people I met in the business and the history passed down to me, and the possibilities that pulled me along, gave me the tenacity.

Then everything else blotted out everything that was not possible. I began deliberately to say, "Oh, one can't waste one's life trying to beat down a door that does not seem to open." Or say, "Here's another door. Oh, this is my door. Oh, here I go," and then find that gradually, all kinds of doors begin to open.

Part of the enormous support team—not part of it, the head of it—was to be married. Eventually we learned how to support each other. We learned that I had something to do besides wash dishes and change diapers. He taught me that, and he also taught me a lot about being a woman. After the fights, after the struggles of just being human beings together, I found out that he listened, and that he made certain conclusions that helped me over the traditional humps that I was forced into as a woman. All women have to overcome something. We have to overcome and become. The same thing applies to younger women today, but at a different level. Our men are learning.

MR. DAVIS: But are we learning fast enough? The statistics are that there are more families now headed by single parents than couples. I'm not sure which way the institution is headed. I certainly hope that we do find a way for men and women to be together. I like that way very much. I have learned it, and I would recommend it to all my friends and to all our children. Ruby did emphasize that a relationship is a working proposition. You have to make that sucker work every day. It's not a given. But if you really work at it, sometimes miracles happen, things that you didn't even expect are there. Wow.

Ossie Davis, age 12

*Ruby Dee, age 13, at summer camp
in upstate New York*

One of the things that accounts for the longevity of our marriage was that we were smart enough, whenever possible, to take the family with us wherever we went. They wouldn't have to worry about what Mom and Dad were doing out there. They went with us.

I worked in Mexico and there was an Easter break; the whole family came. I did another film in Rome. There was an Easter break; whole family came. Ruby did work in Ypsilanti, Michigan, one summer; whole family moved out. Ruby went to Hollywood to do *Raisin in the Sun,* the film; whole family moved out. We made it our business to walk picket lines, participate in demonstrations, meetings, freedom dinners, and all, and the whole gang showed up.

MS. DEE: There was this necessity, too. There was no money in benefits at that time. We've since helped influence that, we think. The NAACP didn't have money to pay people. We would bring the whole family since we weren't going to make any money and couldn't hire baby-sitters, and the children had to have dinner. So we brought them all along.

I can't say that people were always glad to see us and all our children, but our children did learn a lot. They liked going out, and that was part of how we learned to "hang together" as a family.

MR. DAVIS: We never put work ahead of family. They were equal.

MS. DEE: But that wasn't always true. We had to work up to that.

MR. DAVIS: What did we do before we got there?

MS. DEE: Well, I grew up in a traditional way, and it took me a long time to get it out of my head that my job was to stay home and look after the kids. If money had to be made, I expected *him* to go out, get a job at the post office, do something.

Later, when a choice was to be made—Do I take that job when the kids are in school and leave him with the kids, maybe get one of our mothers to pitch in, or hire somebody?—I felt very guilty. Some job offers came that I couldn't accept. I didn't go to England, I didn't go to Hollywood.

When we talked about it, he didn't say, "Oh, Ruby, go on. I'll take care of things." Had he done that, I might have done some other things.

MR. DAVIS: I didn't know to do that. I would have done that, had I thought of it.

MS. DEE: But later on, he encouraged me to go back to school. He was the one who made it easier for us to pack up and all go together, and he made the trips back and forth and began to bring the children when I had to work. It was something that we had to learn to do.

MR. DAVIS: One of the things that I learned late, and I'm still learning, was the special difficulty that Ruby had merely because she was a woman.

It's much easier for us men, in part because men basically control the world and reconfigure it to our needs. We think that when our needs are satisfied, that's the whole thing.

The point I'm trying to make is that a part of what I think we need in our society to help preserve marriages is that men should be encouraged to look at the other side of the equation. Society sets things according to the man, and the woman has to adapt. We men just expect that to happen. I learned for various reasons that this is not so, that people have needs and that those needs should be addressed in terms that make sense to them. That affected my behavior as a man, as a father, as a husband, and so I'd like to share that knowledge with anybody who cares. A woman is a woman, and would benefit sometimes from being treated like a woman.

I remember one night, Ruby, we were coming home after a show we'd done. I became aware of why women could be so successful. The discovery was that whereas a man would normally expect that his day would begin at eight o'clock in the morning and would stop at four o'clock in the afternoon, women had the advantage of never stopping. I wasn't dealing with the question of whether it was fair or not.

You know the old saying, "A man works from sun to sun, but a woman's work is never done." I don't know why it was that while standing, waiting for the subway, that insight hit me, that women created for themselves more time to do what needed to be done, and therefore they could live their lives and then their husband's life, and their children's lives too. The unfairness of that didn't strike me at the time. I thought that it was because you all were just smarter than we were.

MS. DEE: It gave you an excuse to put everything onto me!

During the McCarthy period, when so many people in Hollywood lost their jobs and couldn't work anymore, they would come to New York because in New York at least there were some things you could do. Those people from the group theater showed us something. They helped to solidify for us this way of making a living, one person, two people with a notebook. They taught, encouraged, solidified, put a stamp on this business of a people's art. They and teachers who were thrown out of Brooklyn College and other city universities taught us how to survive in difficult times. They helped us solidify our own ideas about struggles, those that we had known as black people. Since I can remember, our lives have been involved with struggle.

I remember my mother taking us by the hand and walking picket lines. I remember standing on street corners listening and looking up at these protesters talking and talking. I remember struggle. I don't even know what life is all about if there is not some kind of struggle involved. So if you don't know struggle, what do you live about, what do you do with yourself if literature doesn't talk about it? What fortunate people we were, because life happened to us with a capital L. It happened around us and with all these marvelous people we met.

As I look now at our children, the only life they know is the life they *see*. It's not what they *know*. It's what they watch on television or what was part of a story. Human reality is what *happened* to us. Our children don't know that. Not that they should know all the ugliness—people with their belongings in the street, bread lines—but with such knowledge, you can put the past in perspective.

MR. DAVIS: We went to Hollywood, but what did we have when we got there? There was Sidney [Poitier], whom we knew. There was Fred O'Neal, whom we knew. There were other performers whom we knew. This was in 1949.

Hollywood, in a sense, opened its arms at last, and we were among the first permitted to come in. That affected us, our relationship to each other, our sense that what we were doing was important.

MS. DEE: I remember going to Hollywood and feeling intimidated, a little bit inferior, thinking I'm a little black girl from Harlem and here are these important people. There were no African Americans in the technical areas; I didn't see any black cameramen or grips or electricians. No makeup artists. No black people in wardrobe.

So my first experience in Hollywood was intimidating. In those days, for example, if it was a modern-day piece, with everyday clothes, you were expected to bring your own shoes, your own dresses. Only if you wore a costume would Hollywood outfit you. I brought my things to California and I distinctly remember—this picture stays in my mind, perhaps until I die—one wardrobe woman picking up my sling pumps and looking at her friend, and then looking up to heaven as if to say, "Get a load of these." And I felt, "Oh my God, were they dirty? Did they stink?" They weren't new, and they said to bring your clothes. The idea that I should have perhaps brought new shoes or some shoes that hadn't been so worn hadn't even occurred to me until this gesture. And it was the same with the clothes. I began to be embarrassed about what I brought and who I was.

They used to do a screening of you, put you up onscreen and analyze your face. Talking about me, they said, "Well, we'll take her eyebrows down a little." I had thick eyebrows; I was relieved; at least they didn't have to take a hatchet to me! I remember feeling so unworthy. And the hair! I dreaded when I went to get my hair done, because I knew they wouldn't know what to do with my hair. They weren't accustomed to dealing with our hair. Some black person on the set came to me and said, "They really should have a black hairdresser, you know," and hipped me to talk to somebody.

I went to the director because I didn't know who else to tell. You don't generally take that kind of information to the director. But he did take care of it, and before I knew it, there was Elizabeth Surcey on the set as our first hairdresser. She took care of me.

Black people had makeup, but black people had not gotten into the makeup department. A man was telling me what a marvelous department it was, saying it was unionized and there were great people there. I said, "Well, are there any black people in the union?" There was a long, long silence, as if to say "union" was the wrong word or something, and he said, "Well, no, there weren't any black people in the union, but it probably was just a coincidence." I replied, "Well, maybe if you spoke up sometime at a union meeting and asked why there weren't different races in the union . . ."

That was my beginning. I began feeling better about everything. I could talk about it, and they knew where we were coming from, these black people from Harlem. I'm still trying to put all that stuff in perspective.

Until you let the bird out of the cage, it never knows what kind of flier it's going to be. You can only appreciate freedom when you finally find yourself in a position where you're rooting for somebody else's freedom, and not worried about your own.

—RUBY DEE

MR. DAVIS: As performers and actors, we took ourselves rather seriously. We saw the racism, what had been done as World War II veterans were coming home. Black soldiers were being lynched, some of them getting killed trying to vote. Isaac Woodard, a soldier on a bus in South Carolina, had his eyes gouged out. We set out to eliminate it. And when the question arose, politically, of what to do with the atom bomb—shall we give the secrets to everybody else or keep it for ourselves?—the theatrical community was deeply involved in that struggle. When McCarthy came, we were already in the thick of it. There was no way we could go back.

MS. DEE: To tell you the truth, we worked more after the list and McCarthy than we did before, because there was so much more need politically. This was a time when the conscience of America was being stirred.

MR. DAVIS: We were already self-sufficient, because we relied on that audience that we'd developed. And they were still there and still supportive.

MS. DEE: We always felt that there was someplace in this world for us— we could stand on a street corner, go to a church, and somebody would help us get the next bag of groceries. We never doubted that.

I tell you—what our total life experience has been: a sense that, no matter what, we were not just actors. We were black performers, black people. We belong to a certain constituency. I know who I am; I belong somewhere, and these are my people. That idea of "my people, my people" has always been a part of us. Not to the exclusion of any other people, but there's an identity here.

There's something that unites us in struggle. We have become the elite of the oppressed. We know struggle because we hung in there, not that we won—we're still fighting—but we hung in there. We are African Americans. We are also people who are free, because when you know who you are, you're free.

MR. DAVIS: We were in the right place at the right time. Changes were taking place in the society that affected us as individuals and the group from which we came. These were changes that connoted upward mobility and improvement in our status. The importance of our role as performers of the theater, as a means of carrying forth the message, was beginning to be realized. We were there when the message needed a voice, and a hand, or a foot, and it was our joy and our pleasure, and our great reward, to have done it.

MS. DEE: I say to the young: pursue the vision, pursue life lit by some large vision of goodness, beauty, and truth. And as Gwendolyn Brooks admonished, remember always that we are each other's harvest, we are each other's business, we are each other's magnitude and bond.

MR. DAVIS: My advice would be to stay the course, to stay in the game, not to make hasty decisions, not to be bluffed, to be patient, to learn to wait, and give yourself a second chance.

A relationship is a working proposition. You have to make that sucker work every day. It's not a given. But if you really work at it, sometimes miracles happen, things that you didn't even expect are there. Wow.

—OSSIE DAVIS

CARMEN DE LAVALLADE

Born in Los Angeles, California, on March 6, 1931

Dancer, actor, choreographer

———◆———

Dancer, actor, and choreographer Carmen de Lavallade did not align herself with any one dance or theater company, and as a result she became an especially sought-after artist. For her talents in an off-Broadway performance, she received the Clarence Bayfield Award. Roles were created for her by choreographers including Glen Tetley and John Butler. As a dancer, she has performed with the Lester Horton Dance Theater, the Metropolitan Opera, and the Alvin Ailey Dance Company. Her film credits include Carmen Jones; *Duke Ellington's* A Drum Is a Woman; Odds Against Tomorrow *with Harry Belafonte; and, in 1999,* Big Daddy. *A former professor at the Yale School of Drama, she received an honorary doctor of fine arts from the Boston Conservatory of Music and was the director of dance at Adelphi University, on Long Island. While maintaining her presence onstage, de Lavallade continues to choreograph and star in various theatrical productions.*

I started working with dance seriously when I was about fourteen, which is usually rather a late start for most dancers. I wasn't really interested in ballet dancing per se. I was more interested in the contemporary. Janet [her cousin Janet Collins, an accomplished ballerina] didn't have any problem with her feet, and her legs were just gorgeous. I didn't go toward the ballet because my body was not as comfortable with it, although I liked it a lot.

Back then, so few of us were allowed to take ballet. Body typing by race was a way of keeping people away, I think. In John Martin's *Book of Dance,* published in 1963, he wrote that "the black dancer, by virtue of physical characteristics, could not look right dancing ballet."

My body was not the easiest to move. I was not that stretched. I really had to work hard at it. I was long. I had long lines, so I could create an illusion, but I really had to work at it. Sometimes I had people around me who could dance rings around me physically, but I just went in another direction. Having wonderful people give me the imagery gave me something to work with.

I was more interested in the internals of dance, what the movement is *saying,* not what it's doing. I don't like to see transitions. I don't want to see the mechanics. I was more interested in [the choreographers'] vision and what they wanted out of a piece. During that time there were more narrative [dance] works. Now everything is very abstract. I liked working in narration.

I do like the abstract, though. I'm learning to work in it. But you have to have an image of something. I don't think you can do anything without an image. You have to have some point of reference.

If I had stopped to listen to what people said, I would not have done what I did. I was too involved in doing what I was doing. I have a very quiet determination. I just go on and do.

I got to the Met. Following Janet was really nerve-wracking, because it [the Metropolitan Opera] was more balletic. I thought, "Oh, dear."

I tried to make it my own. I was not trying to be, I could not possibly be, Janet. [Modern-dance pioneer] Lester [Horton] told me, "You know you." When I learned Salome, a part Bella [another dancer] had learned previously, he said, "You cannot do what Bella did, and she cannot do what you can do. So there's no competition." He was a choreographer who would change something to suit me when he knew my body wouldn't do it. There were also things that he would never put on Bella that I can do. That gave me a freedom, a respect and a freedom to say, "Hey, I will do it the way I do it. It might not be the way somebody else did it, but I will make something out of it." I would try to create something that was my own. I would make something of the movement they gave me that I felt comfortable with. It seemed to work.

In the '50s all kinds of dance companies were going and everybody shared people. It was wonderful. You kept working with different kinds of people, different kinds of movements and choreographers and their visions. I liked the freedom. I had no problem hopping from one to the other. I found it fascinating. It was not like you were working with the Martha Graham Company all the time, so you only moved one way. Whatever they gave me, I would do.

[Geoffrey and I] just kind of hit it off. Who knows how things work? Bango, there it was, but we've been together forty-seven years.

He's been my champion. I down myself sometimes, and he's been my fan. And I've been his fan. I don't know many married people whose husbands or wives will let each other go flying off in different directions. And the schedules that we keep! We share a lot of respect.

He produces wonderful things. He has a great eye, and I learned an enormous amount from him. And I hope he's learned a lot from me, too. Life is what it is; there are ups and downs, and you butt heads and all that, but, hey, that's living.

Two months after I had Leo [their son], I was dancing again. Poor Leo. God bless him. What a great kid. I didn't have all this care, physical therapy, that kind of stuff. I just got out there and did it. Dancers have that attitude. Most dancers say, "You go and you do your work." You juggle because your life is like that anyway. [My son] would come to rehearsals. It was divine. Once I was working with John Butler, and I'd have to carry Leo and my bags up five flights of stairs to John's studio.

John was from Greenwood, Mississippi—such a gentleman. His two leading ladies were ladies of color, Mary Hinkson and me. His mother, Miss Minnie, was in the back watching a basketball game. She put Leo on her lap and sipped her glass of bourbon while we were rehearsing. It was the most divine thing I'd ever seen. When I ran out of diapers, she used John's wonderful towels from Gucci, Pucci, or somewhere. It was wonderful. [Dance] kept my sanity; movement, something for the body to do, kept my sanity.

Art is a funny thing. It's so vast, and there are so many possibilities; it's just endless. The more that I see, the bigger it gets. That's what I like about it. I don't like to stay in one kind of mold too long. It's wonderful to take on a challenge, whether you succeed or not. Failures sometimes are good experiences; humiliating, but very good experiences. They're necessary.

Art is so fantastic because the mind is so remarkable. We keep inventing new things; nothing is repeated. That's what art is. Human nature is that way. We have so many misunderstandings because everybody wants to

Carmen de Lavallade, age 5, Los Angeles

think that theirs is the only way. Nature is not like that at all. It consists of all kinds of variations on themes.

No repetition for me. When I'm working on a piece, repetition is creating more. The more I play [a role], the richer it gets, the more I find in it. I never stop working on anything.

You cannot freeze anything in time. Otherwise it becomes dead. I just recently did choreography, after all these years. When I was at Yale Rep[ertory], Robert Brustein made me choreograph and stage pieces for the plays. I said, "I can't do that." And he said, "Yes, you can." I appreciate that.

Problem solving is what the theater and dance are about. We're doers.

You set a task for yourself. Now how do you do it, how do you get it, how do you put it onto its final whatever? And is it ever final? Some dancers go back and change everything. The beautiful thing about art is that you are who you are now, and you create who you are now. Whatever is happening now feeds you. So art is going to change.

This would be a dead world without the arts. During the wars, when we didn't have the arts, everything was dead. The minute we brought the arts back, things started to live again. It is an absolute physiological, emotional necessity. I have seen people's lives changed because of the arts. It is something in the human psyche that is absolutely necessary. So-called primitive societies knew that. Modern man has gotten away from it, much to the detriment of the young people. When they took all the arts out of the schools— trouble! Now they have nowhere for that energy to go. Young people have to get rid of that energy. That's what the arts provide. They're writing graffiti on the walls! I don't like seeing it on the walls. I think it should be on canvases.

I got a letter from a lady who was in a wheelchair. She said, for a few minutes at a performance, I was her; she was dancing; she was out of that wheelchair. I thought, "I've done my job." That's what I am here for. I make people feel good.

When young dancers come up to me and say, "I learned so much from watching you," it's wonderful. I don't feel like I'm an older person. I don't feel anything of age. Every age has its own story to tell. Younger people and older people are beginning to blend, and it's really nice. Dance is becoming very intergenerational. We really enjoy working with each other.

My advice [to young African American performers] is be who you are and keep your mind on what you're doing. Never let it [race] get in your way. If you're not right for a part, you're not right for a part. There are times now when I can't get jobs because my hair is too straight and I'm too fair. If I go mumbling about it, that's no good. That doesn't solve it. Go someplace else. There are hundreds of things to do.

We have to get out of thinking, "I'm this and I'm that."

Don't read critics, because they stunt your growth. I never read reviews. You're never the same, so who can criticize you? Tomorrow you're going to be different.

Do the best you can with what you've got; be yourself.

Create your own persona and be faithful to it. I'm not going to say it's easy. It's very hard. The arts [are] a very hard, tough world, and you have to be able to take the knocks. That's why I don't read critics. You must keep your mind on what you're doing. [Knowing yourself] makes you strong and gives you an understanding of people, because you're around people all the time.

Watch out for people who take your mind off what you're doing, telling you what to wear, what to this, what to that. Get yourself down to bare bones and see if you can stand on your own two feet without all that other stuff. What's going to happen when you don't have computers and all that kind of stuff? When the electricity goes off, I can pick up a pencil. There's independence there. Train yourself the other way, too, because you don't know what life is going to bring you.

Develop your way of looking at things, and don't let people tell you how you're *supposed* to look at something. You must learn to protect yourself. Balancing the old with the new is your protection.

GEORGIA SMITH DICKENS

Born in Atlanta, Georgia, on December 24, 1920

Retired educator, community volunteer

Selected and interviewed by
NVLP Fellow Daria Grayer, Spelman College

———•———

Georgia Dickens taught in the Atlanta Public School System for more than forty years before retiring in 1985. A dedicated educator and community volunteer, she worked with the Alliance Children's Theater Guild in Atlanta and presently serves on the Community Relations Committee for the High Museum of Art, also in Atlanta. In honor of her many contributions to the community, she was awarded the Certificate of Achievement for Civic Service from the Carter Center in 1991, and the Spelman Alumnae Achievement Award in 2001. For her work with the Alliance Children's Theater Guild she received the Paul Newman Award.

She and her husband, Robert Dickens, were married forty-five years before he passed away in 1985.

My grandfather was a contractor, so I was born in a thirteen-room house that he had built for my grandmother. We lived there with them until I was in my teens, because my father was pastoring here and there. My father wasn't settled in a church where we could all be together and leave my grandmother's home until 1933. I dearly loved early childhood because I came in contact with so many of the Atlanta University professors.

My grandfather was killed by a trolley in 1921, leaving my grandmother a widow at an early age. She would rent rooms to the college professors. I was surrounded and taught by professors as I was growing up. They were a part of my discipline, my coming and going. Years later, when I entered Spelman, some were still there.

There were four of us children and my parents. I was born in 1920. The Chadwick was an orphans' home, right on Spelman's campus. It had a school, and I attended it until I was twelve, though I was not an orphan.

George Kelsey and others would say, "Come go to school with me today." I got involved in and admired everything they were doing. Even Dr. Hope, who was president of Atlanta University, and his wife stayed with my grandmother before they built that Atlanta University home.

It's like Hillary Clinton says, it takes a village to raise a child. All of these people were most influential in my early childhood and rearing. It was just like a family situation. They were role models, particularly George Kelsey. He was professor of religion at Morehouse, and he'd sit down with us and just chat, and try to guide us, or help my mother because my father was often out of town. I would listen to him, and tried to emulate as much as possible. I worshipped [those professors]. They gave good advice.

All I can remember is being surrounded by people who were my mentors. I am so privileged; there was never anything tragic. I was too young to know my grandfather had passed. Everything looked like it started and progressed, got better and better. I remember learning about the riots that had happened earlier; I've forgotten the exact year of the riots. I've never heard why it didn't come up in my family. But it was something that frightened us because it took place up and down James P. Brawley Drive. People were throwing rocks and everything.

Being surrounded by good people, people who have vision, is part of my success.

They developed my attitude. And my attitude is, I'm here to help. I keep the right perspective.

I was born and reared in an area that was purely academic; we were surrounded by the whole AU Center. Until I started teaching school, I never went beyond Five Points downtown.

That riot is the one bad thing I remember.

You must know who you are, know yourself, have self-esteem, be pleased with yourself. You've got to know what direction you'd like to go and keep focused at all times on that direction.

But you also need to know others. Be mindful of others who may need help. Always be honest with yourself, treat your fellow man right. I don't ever let a challenge bother me. I get to work with the challenge, and most times I can solve it. If I can't solve it, I find the resources to help me solve it.

Respect is the most important thing. You must respect yourself. You must respect others. Especially respect your parents. I cannot understand children who say, "I'm not doing that. Don't you tell me this," to anybody who is older than they are. Elders are historians. We have much to say. I'm not an old person who gripes, not even about my aches. I keep a positive attitude and keep an open mind. I am not going negative. I'm always going to be positive. I stay on a positive plane by thinking, "How can I get on that telephone and call somebody and make her feel good?"

When those younger girls come over here and get me, they say I walk faster than they do! I'm hopping around. I'm doing the electric slide better than they are!

I just love people. I'm a people person. I give of myself.

DAVID DINKINS

Born in Trenton, New Jersey, on July 10, 1927

Attorney, former mayor of New York City (1990–93)

———◆———

David Dinkins was sworn in as mayor of New York City on January 1, 1990. He was the first African American in history to hold that position. "We are all foot soldiers on the march to freedom," he said in his inauguration speech.

As mayor, Dinkins founded the Black and Puerto Rican Legislative Caucus of New York State, and created the office of Special Commissioner of Investigations for schools, as well as Beacon Schools, a system of after-hours youth centers. He also initiated an all-civilian police-complaint review board. Long an outspoken opponent of apartheid in South Africa, he pushed the city to divest $500 million in pension fund stocks from companies that did business in South Africa, and helped pass a bill that allowed the city to rate banks on their opposition to apartheid.

Dinkins focused on making improvements for city residents on issues such as drug abuse, HIV/AIDS, affordable housing, and better schools. His criminal justice plan, "Safe Streets, Safe City: Cops and Kids," reduced crime and, through its youth programs, expanded opportunities for New York City's children.

Dinkins is now a member of the faculty at Columbia University's School of International and Public Affairs. He remains active in New York City politics.

My mother and father separated when I was six or seven years old, and my mother came here to New York from Newport News, Virginia, to live with her mother. My mother and my grandmother were domestics who cooked and cleaned for a dollar a day during the Depression years of the early '30s. We lived in Harlem and moved a lot. When the rent was due, it was deemed time to move.

I was poor, but I didn't know it. My clothes were clean because my mother and grandmother scrubbed them. I never went to bed hungry. I had a good time. I had toys to play with because when the white children got through with their toys, my mother and grandmother brought them home to me.

I always thought my mother and father would get back together. They always had a very civil relationship. When I was in junior high school, I went to Trenton and lived with my father. He was better off financially. Then my father remarried, and I thought I would die. My world had come to an end. I was crushed because I knew my mother and father would never get back together. But my stepmother was a wonderful, amazing woman. A schoolteacher, she taught English and drama in the Trenton Public School System for forty years. She was, in a sense, like another mother. When I got married, my wife's father was like another father to me. So I've been very fortunate in life.

David Dinkins, Howard University, 1950

My mother didn't live to see me become mayor. She always encouraged me. Whatever I did was all right: if I got one A instead of two, that was okay. My father was the same way, but set more of an example of success. He started off as a barber with a one-chair barbershop, but it was *his* chair; he owned the place. He eventually expanded to four chairs. He went to beauty school to [learn how to] do women's hair and did quite well; then rented out the barbershop and became an insurance and real estate broker. He was forever going to school and improving himself. He never went beyond high school and he never got any other degrees, but he got a lot of training, and, by example, taught me an awful lot.

I will never forget the day I was inaugurated as mayor. I gave a long speech, about half an hour, using a TelePrompTer and when I got through, my father said, "Gee, Dave, great speech and no notes."

I said, "Pop, I've got to tell you, I read from a TelePrompTer."

But he always encouraged me, and never ever put me down.

I say to people all the time that nobody gets anywhere alone. When the Kennedys were killed, and Malcolm X and Martin Luther King, people asked, "Where are our leaders?" I said, "We've got lots of leaders." If you're super of a building with six apartments and people listen to you, then you, too, are a leader. Not every leader has great charisma, will be nationally known, or even known citywide. But we have many leaders. A leader, first of all, by definition, must have followers. If nobody's following you, you aren't a leader. A person who watches which way people are going and runs ahead of them saying, "Let me lead my followers," isn't a leader.

But we have many very fine leaders in lots of disciplines and endeavors and we ought to appreciate them. Some will get more attention than others, of course.

And leaders are selected by those they lead. Keep in mind that they came to Martin Luther King and said, "We need you to lead the Montgomery bus boycott." He rose to the occasion.

But there were also others with him: Wyatt T. Walker, who today is pastor of Canaan Baptist Church of Christ in Harlem, New York; Andy Young, who was at Howard with me. He was a couple of years behind me, but we were good friends. I was a dean of probates when he became an Alpha; we laugh about it to this day.

You have to have faith in yourself and faith in those with whom you are working to be a leader.

I've got to tell you, a lot of times, late at night and in the cool, gray light of dawn, it's your family that enables you to lead. My wife and my children have, despite some rough times, always been supportive of me. That helps you face the crises. Any mayor faces tough stuff, but particularly the mayor of New York City. It is the toughest job and the best job for someone who likes public service. The only better job is president of the United States.

I appreciate my family, especially my wife. She has tolerated me all these years. I love to tell the story about when I was mayor and we saw a fellow digging a ditch. I said, "Joyce, isn't that the fellow you used to date?"

I'm not knocking ditchdigging. I have dug ditches, worked in factories, parked cars, washed dishes, waited tables: I've had all kinds of jobs. When I was about eight or nine years old, people used to sell fruits and vegetables from pushcarts at 125th Street and Eighth Avenue. They wouldn't give you a shopping bag—you had to buy one—so I used to buy shopping bags [at] three for a nickel and sell them at two cents apiece. If I sold one to somebody I knew, I'd retrieve it, smooth it out, and resell it. So I'm not knocking ditchdigging. But I said to Joyce, "That *is* the fellow you used to date."

She said, "Yeah, as a matter of fact it is."

I said, "See, if you'd married him, you'd be the wife of a ditchdigger."

She said, "No, if I'd married him, *he'd* be mayor."

DAVID DRISKELL

Born in Eatonton, Georgia, on June 7, 1931

Art historian, curator, professor

David Driskell, internationally acclaimed art connoisseur, curator, scholar, artist, and professor, is one of the world's leading authorities on the subject of African American art. Born in Eatonton, Georgia, in 1931, Driskell has contributed significantly to art history scholarship and the role of the black artist in American society. He has authored five exhibition books on the subject, coauthored four books, and published more than forty catalogues on exhibitions he has curated. As an accomplished artist, his work has been exhibited throughout the United States, in Europe, and in Africa. His primary media are painting and collage, though he has also worked in printmaking, drawing, and sculpture.

Driskell received his undergraduate degree in art from Howard University in 1955 and a master of fine arts degree from Catholic University in 1962, both in Washington, D.C. His interest in art history led to postgraduate study at the Netherlands Institute for the History of Art in The Hague, and further study of the black diaspora in Europe, Africa, and South America.

Much of Driskell's career has been dedicated to promoting greater recognition of the rich history and contributions of African American artists. In 2000 President Clinton awarded him a National Humanities Medal, recognizing his efforts to expand, support, and contribute to this country's understanding of the humanities.

Passionate about the preservation of African American art, Driskell has played a key role in assisting many institutions and individuals in assembling collections that celebrate the varied history of the African diaspora.

Driskell's teaching career spans nearly fifty years, beginning at Talladega College in 1955. He later taught at Howard University and Fisk University and served as visiting professor of art at Bowdoin College, the University of Michigan, Queens College, and Obafemi Awolowo University, in Ile-Ife, Nigeria. In 1995 Driskell was named Distinguished University Professor of Art at the University of Maryland, College Park. He retired from teaching in December 1998. Three years later the University of Maryland established the David C. Driskell Center for the Study of the African Diaspora, honoring Driskell for his many contributions to the field. The center provides future generations with the opportunity to study Africa and the African diaspora from multidisciplinary perspectives.

Driskell continues to work as a practicing artist, curator, collector, and consultant.

My father was an African Methodist Episcopal minister. I was born in the parsonage of Hunt's Chapel A.M.E. Church. When I was five and a half years old, we moved to Polkville, a little town in western North Carolina, in what most people call Appalachia. We didn't actually live in town, we were way out in the sticks. We joined the rest of my mother's family who had migrated to western North Carolina and became farmers. They moved further down in the plateau region; we were literally in the mountains—real Appalachia, Rutherford County. The two black high schools there were very small; each had four rooms. There were about fifteen white high schools, all with big facilities, some with as many as one hundred rooms.

I attended a one-room school from elementary up until what would be considered middle school, and then we had three rooms. To go to high school, I had to ride a total of seventy miles a day to the nearest black high school. I had to get up at four o'clock in the morning, pitch-dark, to get this bus to school. Very often I was the only person on the bus until we came to the next town. People were trying to scratch out a living as farmers on the hillsides and would keep their kids home. But my father was always determined that I would go to school. He said the only way out is through education.

When he moved to North Carolina, he became a sharecropper because there were no A.M.E. churches in that area. They were Methodist Episcopal and C.M.E., Colored Methodist Episcopal. Methodists don't affiliate across their denominations, so instead, he became a Baptist minister when we moved to North Carolina. To make a living, he was a farmer on the side, a sharecropper. We rented a house and land from local whites; planted cotton, corn, and peas. We also had our own garden of potatoes and okra and other vegetables. We were self-sufficient, but there was very little money cleared at the end of the year from the sale of the cotton, because we had to pay for our rations, our food, during the year. Had my father not been literate and able to count, we would have had nothing. The order of the day was for whites to cheat blacks out of everything. But [my father] was very astute and outspoken. He managed to save a little money from the farming and his ministry. He also had an arsenal of guns and pistols. He let us know they were for our protection.

He told us a story once—but he was really talking about himself—about a lady, one of his parishioners he went to visit. He said he walked in the house and on the coffee table was a shotgun and a pistol. He said, "Sister Smith, why do you have this pistol here? Why do you have this shotgun?"

She said, "I have them here to help out the Lord in case He needs help."

He had four churches. Each Sunday he would go to one church, preaching in Tryon, North Carolina, one Sunday; in Gaffney, South Carolina, one Sunday; in Ellenboro, North Carolina, one Sunday; and in Lattimore, North Carolina, one Sunday. I was very aware of [the separation of the races] because we went to separate schools, attended separate churches. Yet there was a mixture on a social level that most people in the North would never think took place in the South. At one time, my father was the only person in the community who had a car, and local whites would come to him on Saturday and—they weren't terribly respectful, never addressing him as "Reverend Driskell" or "Mr. Driskell," but they'd say "Preacher"—say "Preacher, can we borrow your car to go to town?"

The town was eighteen miles away. Daddy, being very considerate and kind, usually said yes. It always all but infuriated me because it was the time I should be learning to drive, and here's somebody off with the car, going to shop. But it was that kind of cooperative spirit. He had both a spirit of militancy and, at the same time, let's be friendly and cooperative. I remember his sermons being social as much as religious, telling people to buy land, to buy homes. He would always say, "Buy land, they aren't making any more. Buy your home, if you can. Vote." This was all mixed into his sermons. Luckily we were in a region where black voting was tolerated. And I say luckily because in the county south of us and into South Carolina, black people were afraid to go to the polls. They didn't give you a hard time in Rutherford County if you attempted to vote.

My father was a no-nonsense person. He couldn't stand for people to waste time. He wanted me to read when I had leisure time. When I was in the fifth grade, he gave me a book, *Basic Teachings of the Great Philosophers*. That's when I first read about Plato and Socrates. I didn't know who they were, but I had to read about them. It helped inculcate in me a desire to learn. He knew that it would, even though he himself was not an educated man. He only went through the sixth grade. But he wrote well and he did a little painting. He was adamant about my schooling and my learning to read because of his father, who was born a slave in 1862 and became a Methodist minister. He was perhaps even more erudite than my father. With only a third-grade education, he taught school. He had beautiful penmanship. We used to ask Daddy why Grandpa spoke so funny; he would shoo us off, or slap us. Depending on where you lived, people interacted across color lines, as they did back in the mountains, because you had to depend on each other to survive back there.

We are able to trace our grandfather's lineage back to Ghana, West Africa, because the crafts that my grandfather did were African in origin. And at the age of seven, I saw him practicing those crafts—and as late as the 1940s, when he came to visit us in North Carolina.

He made ornamental collars for horses, working in the fields, and mats for tables and doors from the bark of the tulepo or poplar tree. He stripped the tree of its bark in long strips of ten or twelve feet. He took the bark to a stream that he would dam up to create a little pool, and he would place it there for twenty-one days. He was very exacting about that. At twenty-one days, it had to come out. As it came out, he would lift it up layer by layer, like sheets of paper. Then he would braid it into three or five braids, and would make ornamental things.

[My grandfather didn't talk about slavery per se], he just talked about the bad times, as he called them. He lived during Reconstruction and he felt the weight of slavery. To him, I guess, repression was just life. But he always had this great hope of the better day. I suppose that was one of the reasons he went into the ministry.

In addition to having to read philosophy books, I had to read the Bible every night. My father would give me a quarter if I committed a certain passage in the Bible to memory. He offered me a dollar to memorize the first Psalm. To this very day, I can recite it word for word. I got that dollar. My father wasn't stern all the time; he was a very loving man. He would take me around the community with him, proud of me because I was the only son. My three sisters were older than I.

My mother was a loving, caring, hugging mother. She was proud of the fact that she had a son, and by her definition I was the smartest child in the world. I wasn't that smart, but she thought so. She gave me self-worth. She would tell me, "You can be anything you want to be; you're as good as anybody. Don't ever let anybody tell you you're not as good as they are because of your color. You can do what they do, or you can do better." She would also say, "You *have* to do better." One of our neighbors was white and had a son, Jimmy. "It's all right for Jimmy to make Cs, but you can't make Cs. You

David Driskell, age 15, as a youth in North Carolina, 1947

have to make As," she said, "because Jimmy will have his place in the world, but you've got to fight for yours."

My mother was a quilter. She did strip quilting and other needlecrafts. I was always interested, and she'd say, "No, boys can't do that." I would see her crocheting and say, "I want to learn to crochet." She said, "No, no, not boys." So I would crochet behind her back. I learned to do all those things—sew and crochet.

I was always observing people. I wanted to learn what made them tick. One person in the community painted, one black man, and he painted rather well. He was a deacon in my father's church. He painted landscapes. I was fascinated by people who had various creative interests.

[As mentioned before], my father had a church in Tryon, North Carolina. Nina Simone came from that same community. But she was not a member of his church. I recall seeing her at Fisk University when I was a professor there in the late '60s and she came to perform. When I was introduced to her, she asked me, "Are you Reverend Driskell's son?" She sang gospel in Tryon.

In those days if you changed from singing gospel to the blues or jazz, you were an outcast. She was probably thinking, "What would Reverend Driskell say?" She used to play the piano in all those churches around Tryon.

As early as the second and third grades, my teachers observed my desire to draw. I had just one teacher through the third grade, we were all seven grades in one small room. I could draw. I could copy things from books. My teacher, Miss Edna Freeman, encouraged me to draw. At the end of the school session, at the end of May every year, we had what we called commencement. It had nothing to do with graduation. It meant going to the big brick black school—four rooms!—with an auditorium, displaying our art, having a spelling bee and other competitions. I was always called on to do the artwork. That's how I got started. The first time, I was in the third grade. The teacher had me copy a whole book, *Sleepytown Wakes Up.* I did all of the pictures, and we submitted that as an original work of art. We knew nothing about plagiarism! When I went to the three-room school, the word had preceded me—David can draw. I had to do all of the drawings for all three teachers in the school. I did the drawings for the stage, and all activities. When I went to high school, the same thing. I was always encouraged.

Stay the course but look at it with the notion that you have a mission to heal. You have a mission to be part of the healing process. That you have no right to be a part of the problem. We're too far along.

[My father] told us a story once . . . about a lady, one of the parishioners he went to visit. He said he walked in the house and on the coffee table was a shotgun and a pistol. He said, "Sister Smith, why do you have this pistol here? Why do you have this shotgun?"

She said, "I have them here to help out the Lord in case He needs help."

—DAVID DRISKELL

KATHERINE DUNHAM

Born in Chicago, Illinois, on June 22, 1909

Choreographer, dancer

———————

Katherine Dunham is best known for her groundbreaking choreography based on African American, Caribbean, West African, and South American sources. For more than thirty years, Miss Dunham maintained the only self-subsidized dance troupe in the world. She financed her business with nightclub engagements, Hollywood Bowl appearances, and concerts in more than fifty-seven countries around the globe. She choreographed for film and television. Miss Dunham opened her own dance schools in Paris, Stockholm, Rome, New York City, and eventually St. Louis, home of the Katherine Dunham Museum and the Katherine Dunham Centers for the Humanities.

She is frequently called upon to lecture and teach at universities, including her alma mater, the University of Chicago.

The meeting of art and science is very important to me. I'm glad to have been one of the forerunners of that fusion. But nothing satisfied me as much as the investigation of dance, the participation in dance, the creation of dances, and helping develop dancers.

At the University of Chicago, I decided that I would not become an anthropologist, although I knew I would always love anthropology. When I decided, "Dance is what I want to do, but I will not give up anthropology," the two of them came together.

Most of the time when I was studying anthropology I thought of myself as a researcher. I wanted to travel, know more, see more about people, and go into their lives. When I first went to the Caribbean I felt that I had come home. I never felt like a stranger, an outsider, especially after I was initiated into the Vodoun religion in Haiti. I felt that these were people I knew but should know more about. Whether it was a meal at somebody's house, some different food I wanted to know how to make, or going to a ceremony, I felt, "I belong here."

I felt there were bridges that I was destined to cross and ties I wanted to make to bring those people more into our lives. I wanted to bring them into our whole notion of being black. I wanted them to know about Africa, of course, but I wanted them to know about North America too.

In Jamaica the Maroon people had never had anyone from the outside spend the night. Persons had been there during the day, but no one had ever spent the night. That was my *Journey to Accompong,* my stay with them. It was my interest in being a part of them that made them open up to me.

It's good to know that something needed to be done, and that you did it. For me it was good to know that these people needed to know more about themselves, and the world needed to know more about them. Those things I was able to do, and I felt very accomplished in doing them.

I was once asked what I would like to have on my tombstone, and I replied, "She tried." Always try. Seldom have I not tried to get anything that

Katherine Dunham, in costume for a performance, 1945

I really wanted. If I really wanted it, I would try. And almost 100 percent of the time, it would happen.

I have not been able to thank the people who have been an influence in my life who've helped me. I regret not having kept better accounting of these people so that I can thank them. Sometimes I think of making a blanket statement: "Everybody who helped me, thank you." But that isn't enough. I have not taken the time to stop and say thank you to people who were important in my life and who really helped me. Thank you is important.

We are accustomed to playing games. We are accustomed to procrastinating. It's too bad because it wastes time. Be demanding. Don't be complacent.

I feel so battle-weary. It shouldn't be necessary to work so hard to achieve things that are so obviously right, like the recognition of one's fellow man, but most people don't live by that principle. If people realized how much they could do, they would do it. Most people don't realize it; they don't realize that while you can't change a whole community, you can't change the world, you can make a change in your own small universe. Most don't know that they have a universe, and that's the trouble. We don't know how vast and how great our capacities are.

Patience and flexibility are very important, but action is most important. No longer can people sit down and let somebody else do it. Young people coming along have to *do,* and they have to learn how to find themselves in doing. In nondoing they lose themselves. The advice I give is to stop and look at yourself carefully.

Accept wisdom now.

To accept words of wisdom, you have to discriminate. Learn how to discriminate, what to do and what not to do, just as you would what to eat and what not to eat. If you can do this, you are one of the stones that will be the future foundation for humanity.

NORMAN C. FRANCIS

Born in Lafayette, Louisiana, on March 20, 1931

President of Xavier University of Louisiana

Selected and interviewed by
NVLP Fellow Jeanine Price, Xavier University

—◆—

After graduating from Xavier University in 1952, Norman C. Francis became the first African American to be accepted to Loyola Law School in New Orleans, Louisiana, and was the school's first African American graduate in 1955. After two years in the Army, Dr. Francis returned to Xavier in 1957, where he spent eleven years in various university positions, including director of development and executive vice president. In 1968 he assumed his current position as university president. Over the course of his career, he has also served as an adviser to five presidential administrations and served on several national boards, including the board of directors of the American Council on Education. He and his wife, Blanche, have been married forty-eight years.

$\mathcal{M}$y dad believed that you had to work and you had to be willing to work with your hands. His phrase was, "You will make a living working with your hands, but you'll make money working with your head." I couldn't work with my head while I was in school, so I worked with my hands.

[When I was fourteen years old], I worked on the main street in town in what was called a shoeshine parlor. I was making decent money, ten or fifteen cents for each pair of shoes. I learned a lot about people. I saw every kind of individual who sat on that shoeshine stand. And I could tell the ones who respected me as an individual, and those who did not respect me because I was shining shoes. In many ways, I was being educated. My family background gave me the understanding that even if you don't have a lot of money, make the best of what you have. Never complain about what you have, and do the best with it. Be willing to work, even if it means working with your hands. And always respect people that work, no matter what background they are from.

My father left his work at the railroad and became a bellhop in the hotel in the city. He opened his own barbershop. He became an entrepreneur. I remember distinctly, every night he'd come home and he would write in a little book. He recorded what he made. I've looked in that book and it was perhaps $2.50 or $3.50 a day. You could get a haircut for ten or fifteen cents at that time.

I used to deliver my daddy's lunch at the barbershop. And I, of course, got my hair cut by him on days when things were slow. I hung around the barbershop whenever I could. I learned to play checkers with old men who were experts. Some of them were Pullman porters who worked on the railroad. I lived in Lafayette. The trains left from New Orleans and made stops in Lafayette, Beaumont, Houston, all the way to Los Angeles. Many of the porters would "deadhead." They'd stop in Lafayette, then pick up the next train. The porters stayed across the street from my dad's barbershop. They couldn't stay in the hotels. The porters slept at a flophouse, and they'd come over to my dad's barbershop. The funeral home director and insurance man, the middle-class blacks who had money, would also always be there. I learned to play checkers and those old men in the barbershop taught me: Don't ask anybody to give you a break. You make your breaks.

What I do here at Xavier has roots in what I learned in checkers, namely, always think first and get advice. Ask the question: if I do that, what happens here or what happens there? What's the next move? Checkers taught me that you have to think about every move you make.

JOHN HOPE FRANKLIN

Born in Rentiesville, Oklahoma, January 2, 1915

Historian, educator, author

———◆———

Noted historian, scholar, author, and professor John Hope Franklin is highly regarded for his efforts to promote racial understanding and reconciliation. He graduated from Fisk University and earned his doctorate in history from Harvard University. He credits both schools with helping him achieve the scholarly discipline that allowed him to reshape the way African American history is understood and taught. A prolific author, his literary landmark, From Slavery to Freedom, *is now in its eighth edition and has been translated into five languages. In 1997 he coedited with his son, John W. Franklin,* My Life and an Era: The Autobiography of Buck Franklin, *the story of his own father who was an attorney. Through his many books, he has shaped twentieth-century American history with his integrated visions of scholarship and activism, passion and prudence.*

A devoted teacher as well as a historian, Franklin has served on the faculties of several colleges and universities, including St. Augustine's College, Howard University, Brooklyn College, University of Chicago, and Duke University. Franklin has also served on many national commissions and delegations, and was chosen by President Clinton in 1997 to chair the advisory board for One America: The President's Initiative on Race.

Franklin's powerful chronicle of Black America's hard-won progress toward equal rights and status continues to guide us toward a just society. One of the most celebrated historians in the United States, he has been honored with countless awards—among them the Encyclopedia Britannica Gold Medal for the Dissemination of Knowledge, the NAACP's Spingarn Medal, and the Presidential Medal of Freedom.

Dr. Franklin is currently the James B. Duke Professor Emeritus of History at Duke University.

I was born in Rentiesville, Oklahoma, in a village which had no facilities for youth—no parks, no playgrounds. There was no organized recreational life whatsoever. There was school, and Sunday school. There was no library, nothing that could edify a youngster. Nowhere to go; nothing to do.

When I was six years old, my father, a lawyer, moved to Tulsa, Oklahoma, a much larger city, bustling, hustling, growing, and very prosperous in the '20s. We were to move at the end of our school year. My mother was teaching. My sister and I were in school. My older brother and sister were away in private school.

We were all ready to go and have a new life when the race riot engulfed Tulsa. The entire black section of Tulsa was first looted, then burned and bombed. Large numbers of people were killed. My father was kept in a detention center for several days.

For days, we didn't know whether my father was living or dead. Then we got a message that he was alive and well. But everything he owned, except the clothes he was wearing the night of the riot, had been destroyed. He had no money. The house he'd gotten for us to live in was gone. We had to remain in Rentiesville for four more years, years that were very important in my own development. I had no father, except that he visited sporadically, and the responsibility of raising me devolved entirely on my mother. She was equal to the task, I hasten to say. She taught me so much of what I learned in that period, including how to fish, for example. She even invented games for us. We lived out from the village, and the nights were lonely. There was not much to do in the evenings other than read. One of the reasons my eyes are as weak as they are today is that I read too much by lamplight between the ages of six and ten. We had no running water, no electricity, no heat, except from burning logs—we had no coal.

It was a hard childhood. We were essentially latchkey kids, my sister and I. My mother was teaching, not in Rentiesville, but over what we called "the mountains." They weren't mountains, but it was in another section. She went by horse every day. We went to the school in Rentiesville, and would get home before she did.

We had certain duties. We had to get the wood in, clean the soot out of the chimneys of the lamps with newspaper, wash the dishes, and take care of ourselves until my mother arrived home to prepare the evening meal and to see that we got our homework done.

I was studious, but I was also mischievous. I was probably beyond my class in achievement, therefore bored by class, and I got into a lot of trouble. I took a class in auto mechanics in which the teacher said he would give me a B if I would promise not to come to class anymore because I made so much noise. He was disgusted with me and my friends. We were making more noise than the engines in the room.

I never had any dreams of what I wanted to do. I knew I wanted to be a lawyer, that was to emulate my father. By the time I got to high school, the Depression had hit, and we were even more impoverished than we had ever been. We had no Christmas at all. I did not understand the Depression or how poverty happened. I concluded that we were in poverty because my father was a poor businessman, and my real ambition was to go to law school, become a lawyer, and come back and rescue him—give him the opportunity to practice law without having to fret about business. I would do the business and rake in the money.

I did not know about the worldwide Depression, that unemployment was high everywhere, highest among blacks. Nor did I understand that many blacks who were able to have lawyers did not entrust their legal problems to African American lawyers, because African American lawyers did not enjoy the respect that they were entitled to in the courts. You're already in jeopardy if you're in legal trouble. Why put yourself in more jeopardy, more trouble, by having a lawyer who enjoys no full respect in the courts, you see? And I did not understand that. I just felt my daddy was a good lawyer but a poor businessman, and then, if I went to law school, and returned to practice with him, we'd get on Easy Street immediately.

I understood what racism was, but I grew up without fear. This was particularly true after we moved to Tulsa in 1925.

I knew what racism was but I didn't understand it. The town of Checotah, six miles south of Rentiesville, was where we did our shopping. You'd have to flag the train in a village like that. We stopped the train, got on, and it started immediately. The conductor came back and said, "You can't sit here, you know, this is for white people."

My mother said, "I can't move my children to another car as long as the train's moving."

He said, "Well, I'll stop the train." He stopped the train. They put us off. I began to cry because I had anticipated going to Checotah. "What's the matter? What are you crying for?" Mother said. I cried, "That man put us off the train."

"He was enforcing the law," she said, "and that law is a bad law, because we have as much right to ride that train and to ride anywhere on that train as anybody else does. And don't you cry because of what that law did to you. You must understand that there's no one on that train better than you are. You have as much right as anybody on that train. You want to feel sorry for people like him and oppose laws that are unfair and are unjust."

We'd been to Checotah before. I'd seen white people, and I had observed how black people were treated differently from white people. I knew I could not eat in a white restaurant in Checotah. I knew that I could eat only at my cousin's place. He had a small restaurant, a hamburger stand. I had a hamburger for the first time, and it was a great experience. But the fact that I could not eat at certain places told me that there was something wrong. And the fact that I lived in a town where there were no white people was another indication that racial separation was a reality in our lives. I learned—very early, I don't know quite when—that black people were being lynched.

Yet, I have never felt uncomfortable around people of another race, never. I don't know why. I simply don't look at them as being different. When I was a professor at the University of Chicago, I was lecturing to an undergraduate group of students. (I always insisted on teaching an undergraduate class in Chicago, although I didn't have to.) I was at the front of a very small amphitheater, and the tiers of rows went up to the back of the room. When a person came in the room, they had to come down to sit in one of the rows. Mid-lecture an African American student came in. I had about eight or ten African Americans in this class of sixty or seventy students.

The student stood in the back of the room looking—I did not know what for, but I was lecturing and watching her. And then she saw the row of students where African American students were sitting. Students were all sitting next to the aisle, so she had to climb over the students to get in that row to sit by another African American student. I lost my train of thought. I was absolutely dumbfounded. I could not understand what she was doing or what this meant to her. She might have made herself comfortable anywhere in the room. I did not understand that she got some satisfaction, some comfort, in sitting next to another African American.

When I was in graduate school, I didn't have that problem because there were no blacks in any class that I went to, and I just came in and sat myself down wherever I wanted to.

I was not at all uncomfortable. I thought students ought to feel comfortable. I know that they don't. I know there are reasons why they don't. But I had no reason to feel uncomfortable with my professor, Theodore Currier. I've never had a more natural relationship than the one I had with him. I didn't feel one moment of awkwardness, not at all. It's a credit to him that he was able to achieve the level of trust and confidence I had in him. He certainly inspired it, and caused me to feel absolutely comfortable.

We ate together—not regularly, but whenever we could. He took me riding. He mentored me. Then he pointed me toward Harvard; he very deliberately said, "I want you to go to Harvard." He saw in me the potential to do some things that he hadn't done in his own life. He projected himself into my life. I believe one of his great motivations for bringing Phi Beta Kappa to

Fisk was to get me in Phi Beta Kappa. He expressed such great confidence in me that I moved right on, without any goals. I never have had any goals in life except to do extremely well, as well as I can do. I haven't said, "I'm going to be a professor at this school or that school" or "I'm going to be president of this or that." Never. I'm without ambition in that sense. But I've always worked hard and tried to do the best I could, and I've let the rest take care of itself.

I always believed that education was a great instrument to rectify the ills of society. I wanted to teach society something about itself that it might not know, and I hoped these lessons would be effective instruments for making progress along racial lines. Then I got into research. I liked to read and write, and I wanted to do more. I had published my first book when I was twenty-six or -seven, and I wanted to write another one. I kept on writing and working. I was a young professor, but I kept running to the library. I had a study room down there, [and I was] working every day, trying to educate this country because I thought they were ignorant about race, and about racial relationships in these areas. I got great satisfaction personally out of doing the work. If it would assist us in moving a few notches forward, that was also very good. My motives were not so high-flown as to think that I could change the world by writing another book, but I hoped that some might modify their views and actions.

I'm disappointed that we haven't moved as fast and as far as I would like. I'm disappointed that some people do not regard my books as the truth. I am sobered by the fact that I can write my head off, and there'll be some people who say, "Well, how stupid can you be?" and "Look at Franklin, he doesn't know what he's talking about, this is not going to happen," "This is not going to move the world."

My father was a greater optimist than I am. He thought that I was too young to be so lacking in hope for the future. I kept my hopes under control, enchained, without letting [them] get away from me. I was restrained and said only, "Well, maybe some people will believe [my work], and some people will be changed by what I expose. But I would get great satisfaction even if they weren't, because it's a personal satisfaction that I can achieve [through my writing.]" He thought that was not good, that I should be much more optimistic that mankind would move more rapidly toward perfection. He and I argued this and I said, "You're so romantic, you're just full of imagination. You're soft." We had a wonderful time arguing.

When I was appointed to chair the advisory board on the President's Initiative on Race during the Clinton administration, some thought I had been given the power to solve the race problem. I would point out that I was just making some suggestions to the president on what he ought to do; expectations were high, and therefore large numbers of people were disappointed. I was not disappointed. I was very much heartened because I didn't expect as much as others. Whatever we did to develop promising practices, agencies, and activities, I was very pleased with.

The night before I received the Presidential Medal of Freedom in 1995, I gave a dinner party at the Cosmos Club, in Washington, D.C., to which I have belonged since 1962. I was the first African American member. Some of my friends had never been to the club, and I was showing them around. We got up to the library and I, realizing a member of my party had not yet come, went down the grand staircase to see if I could find this person. When I reached the bottom of the stairs, a woman came to me with her hat check and said, "Here, go and get my coat."

"Madam, if you will present that to one of the attendants at the club, one of the *uniformed* attendants"—and all of the attendants at this club are uniformed—"perhaps you'll get your coat," I said, and walked away thinking,

John Hope Franklin, Fisk University commencement, 1935

"That poor old woman—my God." My picture's hanging on the wall within a few feet of where she spoke to me; I'm the Cosmos Club "Man of the Year."

I'm not distressed or disturbed unduly by this woman. I can multiply her I don't know how many times to get the number of times that I've experienced the same thing in various parts of the United States, from New York City to Oklahoma.

But I have historical perspective. I'm not going to get sick because of that. I've got too much to do, too much to live for, too much to think about. I'm simply going to live my life, and with any extra energy I have, I'll fight American apartheid.

I hope there'll be many more black members of the Cosmos Club—and there are large numbers now—and I hope that there will be so many black achievers that this woman or her descendants will say, "Well, maybe it's late in the day, but maybe I ought to recognize them for what they are— decent, upstanding, high-achieving human beings."

DICK GREGORY

Born in St. Louis, Missouri, on October 12, 1932

Activist, comedian, author

———

Richard Claxton "Dick" Gregory, comedian and civil rights activist, changed the way white Americans perceived African American comedians through his social satire. After a childhood of poverty in St. Louis, Gregory attended college on a track scholarship and later served two years in the Army. In the mid-1950s he began successfully developing his career as a comedian. Gregory also put his convictions into practice by devoting much of his time to the Civil Rights Movement of the 1960s. Gregory made appearances at demonstrations, marches, and rallies throughout the country. In 1966 he was a candidate for mayor of Chicago and in 1968 the presidential candidate of the Freedom and Peace Party. His unsuccessful presidential bid, a write-in effort in most states, garnered some 200,000 votes and substantial media attention. Eventually he quit the nightclub circuit in favor of speaking engagements at colleges, churches, and schools.

Gregory continues to be an outspoken activist for human and civil rights. He is the author of several books, including Dick Gregory's Natural Diet for Folks Who Eat *and his acclaimed 1964 autobiography,* Nigger. *His most recent book,* Callus on My Soul: A Memoir, *was published in 2000.*

*T*he first demonstration that I was involved in was when I was the first Negro to win the high school state championship in the mile. At that time, most Negroes were convinced that genetically we could only run short races. I set the world record in the high school mile, and didn't get credit for it because I was at the Negro meet. We had Negro state meets and white state meets. You can imagine being born, don't know your daddy, in utter poverty. I really resented my mother. I resented the conditions I grew up in. And then one day I did something that no one in the history of the planet had ever done, and I did not get credit for it, either.

So I went down to the board of education and asked the superintendent why. Did they have any doubt [that I set the record]? He said Negro meets don't count, and that's when I declared war on the city. We organized and shut down the school system. It was kind of interesting because they thought it was about a segregated school system. After [the demonstration], I went to jail. The FBI told my mother I was a communist. Two days later, we went back with another demonstration. And the [superintendent] just went off. "Tell me what you want," he said. I said, "I want my record to count." That is when I realized I had the power of the white man. His whole demeanor changed, because the NAACP was part of the march. They were talking about overcrowded conditions in the schools, but they were never able to get a big march off like this. So the superintendent said, "Just a minute." He made a phone call, came back, and signed the executive order. Cross country was integrated right there.

When I got out of the service [Gregory had begun performing comedy in the mid-1950s while serving in the Army], I went to Chicago to hook up with a friend of mine that I'd met in the Army. That was the first time I'd been in a nightclub in my life. In Chicago there were Negro nightclubs and white nightclubs. I went into a club and saw black comedians, the first time I had

Dick Gregory during a track workout, ca. 1952

ever seen a black comedian in my life. And so I went in there and I just said to a friend of mine, "Jesus Christ, what a wonderful way to make a living!"

I just kept talking about it and talking about it, and then the next week I went to this little nightclub, and I lied and told them I was a big comic in from New York. I paid the guy $15 to bring me up and introduce me. I was funny, and they hired me for $5 a night. I go back, and that's when I got a rude awakening that I wasn't funny. I didn't know there was a thing called timing. I didn't know there was a thing called breathing. A singer can almost listen to how much [vocal] training you have had just by the way you pronounce words. Well, that's the same thing with comedy. I didn't know any of this then, but I learned quick.

This is a rule for all comics. Timing comes only from working. Wherever I had to go, pool halls or churches, I had to get the rhythm and timing. Once you learn it, it's like knowing how to ride a bike—you can never unlearn how to ride a bike.

I wrote my autobiography, but [the publishers] wanted a humor book. They didn't say that. They said to me, "Would you do us a favor? Over the weekend, would you name it something humorous?" And what they really wanted me to do was have a humorous name so white folks would see it and think it was not a book about black life in white America. And so I said to my wife, "You know what? Let's take this 'nigger snake' and defang it."

Now the book is mandatory reading in many schools across the country. But people, and rightfully so, were scared to put it in the window because of the title. Even black folks would come in and say, "I'd like to get one of them whatchamacallits of Dick Gregory." But the snake, it was defanged.

The strongest two forces in the history of the planet, of America, have been the black woman and the black church, and I don't think it's an accident. And one day, when we look back into the early days of the Movement, 99 percent of everybody in that movement had "Reverend" in front of their names, and 99 percent in the Movement were not men, it was women, 'cause the men went to work, and it was those sisters that was holding those rallies every day. But when the cameras got there, it turned into a man thing.

When I made the first decision to go, I said to my wife, you probably won't see me no more. When I was in the Army, I was willing to kill someone or die for a racist country that wouldn't give me the time of day. That's insane, that's ungodly, that's unspiritual. If the captain said, "Let's take this hill," I was willing to go. Then, I had no children, I had no wife, but I said to her, "Had you been married to me and had some children nothing would have changed. We're not gonna use our family as a cop-out not to be part of the Civil Rights Movement." Because when you are fighting for America, they don't ask you how will taking that hill affect your family.

When I went down to the South for the first time there were about six hundred cops at the airport waiting for me. It was the first time I really felt like John Wayne. I felt big. I felt big as God. I felt all of these people that I'm scared of, been scared of all my life, they're so frightened of me, and that's when I understood the power of what I was messing with.

Let me tell you about this movement. To see a four-year-old child in jail with me at two o'clock in the morning, I'm embarrassed, I'm insulted, I'm outraged, and I look at him, and I hold him like I was holding a child of mine, and I say, "Why are you here?" And he said, "Teetem." He couldn't even say freedom.

When I go around the world, and look people in the eye, King is there, Malcolm's there, all of the joy of this movement is there. I wouldn't trade that off for nothing; there was such a joy inside of me from this movement. To be out here, committed to this movement, you understand respect.

And so you stop and you think about [how] there will come a day that it won't make a difference. We haven't got there yet. But every little notch is knocking it down and knocking it down. It was something we had to do.

I would say to young folks: don't be in a state of denial about racism and sexism. But don't let it block you. Don't teach your children that you have to be twice as good as a white. That's an awful thing to teach a child. That's like saying, because you're black, white America has a right to change your dollar for 94 cents. We used to get 50 cents. Before that we got nothing. Young folks have to say, "We want a full dollar's change for a dollar, or this cash register will never ring again."

ROBERT GUILLAUME

Born in St. Louis, Missouri, on November 30, 1927

Actor

—◆—

Veteran of stage, screen, and television for more than forty years, Robert Guillaume has endeared himself to millions across America with his humorous, frequently satirical, and always memorable character portrayals.

Guillaume has worked in musicals throughout the country and has toured in Europe. He also made several guest TV appearances, eventually arriving in New York to play one of the lead roles in Broadway's all-black revival of Guys and Dolls. *His interpretation of Nathan Detroit won him a 1977 Tony nomination for Best Actor.*

Perhaps his biggest challenge and triumph onstage came in May of 1990 when he became the only African American to play the lead role in Phantom of the Opera. *Though extremely successful onstage, Guillaume may be best known for his television roles, particularly his portrayal of Benson—the wisecracking, back-talking butler in the hit series* Soap. *He won an Emmy Award for Best Supporting Actor on* Soap *in 1979, and later another Emmy for Best Actor on the spin-off show* Benson. *In the late '90s, Guillaume starred in the witty, fast-paced TV show* Sports Night, *a role that he says was one of his favorites.*

*M*y grandmother used to work in "service," and she never took a backseat to anything. She'd get to her job in the morning, and when I was a kid I'd usually go with her. I'd play with the kids in the neighborhoods of those very wealthy people. I remember the woman who hired her waiting with a cocktail in hand, half tipsy, trying to pretend she wasn't drunk. She began instructing my grandmother on how to load the washing machine.

My grandmother did not suffer fools gladly. She'd let her lecture for a few minutes, and then said, "Now sweetheart, if you want me to do it, I'll do it. If you want to do it yourself, then you don't need me, I'll just leave."

"Oh, no, no, Jeanetta, I want you to put the pillowcases in with the so and so and so and so."

"I told you I'm not going to do it that way," my grandmother said. "I'm going to do it my way or I won't do it."

"Oh, well, have your own way."

That's what was going through my head when I did *Benson*. I knew I was not playing anyone who was inferior. I was a little dicey at first about playing a servant because I know how my people feel about servants. But I had a philosophy that servants were not dumb people. They couldn't be. Maybe some people need to *feel* that servants are beneath them intellectually, certainly financially. But I figured out that, intellectually, they can't be, because you don't want anyone who is intellectually inferior to you serving you, doing things for you, and running your house. You can't have it. They'll burn down the house.

You have to hire someone who's pretty hip because it's an all-encompassing job. The relationship between so-called master and servant has been treated many, many times in films, and it's crazy because things turn around: the guy may hire the servant, but the servant begins to know more than the master.

I worked happily with people who, first of all, had written the character against type. We started to move the character up; he became lieutenant governor, and he was to run for governor had we continued as scheduled. But the producers and the network got mad at each other and yanked *Benson* after a seven-year run. That's a good run.

People ask me if I wouldn't rather be known as an actor than a black actor? I don't understand that question because I don't see any diminution of universality in black people. We are no less universal as representatives of the human race. But unfortunately, many people do and they cannot get away from it. It's unspoken racism. It is the notion that everything has to have the imprimatur of a white person.

I got tired of trying to be all things to all people in acting. I was finally able to renounce that notion. I can't carry that burden.

I do believe in myself. When I began to renounce notions of being a great actor, I began to feel that if I can walk out here and stand in front of the camera, all is right with the world. I must go out in front of the camera, or on the stage, and be totally comfortable. I'm not saying I shouldn't have fear, but I shouldn't fear anyone's opinion of me.

Self-confidence is courage in acting and for black actors especially, because we often work under the assumption that everybody knows more than we do. I have talked to so many black professionals who are afraid to be themselves, to draw on their own knowledge. An actress in a down-home piece had trouble with the lines that go, "You like sweet potato pie—you like sweet potato pie, don't you, honey?" "Yes. I know you do. Uh-hmm. Yeah." "You know, I don't know what's wrong with Pearly. Ever

Robert Guillaume in the Army, 1945

since he came from up North, he got back down here, he's just fidgeting. Fidgeting all over the place."

She was having trouble with the line "You like sweet potato pie, don't you?"

We were being directed by a very nice young man who had a pink sweater wrapped around his neck while directing us. She was giving him the entire interpretation of that line afraid she was going to make a mistake.

I said to her, "You've been in the business thirty years. You know what this line means, don't you?"

"Well, I'm not sure."

"What do you mean you're not sure? What does it say?" Too often black actors are afraid of what they already know. They remember a time when we weren't supposed to know a goddamn thing. It's ridiculous! I just want black people to step into the sunshine.

There was a cutoff date after which I didn't owe any dues. After Martin Luther King Jr. was killed, I didn't owe any more dues. I will walk into the sunshine with you, or you will not be my friend. I will instruct you and you will instruct me. I will learn things from you and you will learn things from me. Otherwise you can't be my friend.

My heart will be gladdened if I get black people to take their place alongside other people, without the need for braggadocio, strutting, and preening.

To young actors: take a look at yourself, assess your positives and negatives, decide on something you really want to do—give it thought, weigh it—then take a chance.

MARCUS GUNTER

Born in Nashville, Tennessee, on January 23, 1918; died on June 17, 2003

High-school band director for thirty-nine years in Nashville, Tennessee;

funeral home director

Selected and interviewed by

NVLP Fellow Cheri Carter, Fisk University

———— ⦁ ————

While serving as a member of the 41st combat engineers in World War II, Marcus Gunter raised his spirits by playing and listening to music. After being discharged from the Army in 1947, he began his thirty-nine-year teaching career at Pearl High School in Nashville, Tennessee. While serving as band director of the symphonic and marching bands, he prepared his students to play for U.S. presidents Eisenhower and Kennedy. He is remembered for his passion for music and commitment to teaching.

I retired from Pearl High as dean of the faculty for student affairs. I was the bandleader for twenty-seven years, and the last twelve years, I was in charge of all student affairs.

Pearl was the only high school in Nashville for blacks. Everybody in

South Nashville came to Pearl, everybody in East Nashville came to Pearl, everybody in Washington went to Pearl. It was a melting pot of all the blacks in Nashville. When Pearl started back in the 1880s and '90s, you had a group of children who were children of freed slaves. Pearl was the first high school for blacks in Tennessee.

Every boy that I had contact with first learned how to dress, how to have shined shoes, how to be polite, and, most of all, be a serious school learner and keep good grades. If a boy was making Cs and Ds, he couldn't play in our band until he could bring up his grades.

Eighty percent of the guys that I taught went on to college. When I became dean of the faculty, I emphasized that the kids had to stay in school. The greatest thing was seeing the students succeed. We had kids at the University of Michigan, Arizona State, Fisk, Harvard. We had kids all over, and that was a great feeling to know that you have kids who had achieved. I have students who still come by to see me. We just had a reunion this year and I guess this whole room was packed with students I had taught. I have their respect and I was able to indoctrinate them into good music. Not rock 'n' roll, but the classics. That is an achievement.

My advice for young people is first of all, they need to stop killing each other. Number two, you cannot achieve without a college education, there's no way. You have to set a goal to find out where the money is and how to get it; not being a crook, but something productive; start a business. And the black young men need to vote. You can't sit home and think somebody's going to give you something, you have to fight for what you get. The young black American has got to like himself, love himself as a person. And then you can make it. But a person's got to have an education.

BARBARA HARRIS

Born in Philadelphia, Pennsylvania, on June 12, 1930

First female bishop of the Episcopal Church

—◆—

Rev. Bishop Barbara Harris holds the distinction of being the first ordained female bishop of the United States Episcopal Church. When she assumed this position in 1989, she broke a 2,000-year-old tradition stretching back to the time of Christ's apostles. Prior to her election in this capacity, she was a civil rights activist, public relations specialist, executive with the Sun Oil Company, executive director of the Episcopal Publishing Company, and a lay minister, priest, and writer.

Although she would not be ordained as a priest until almost forty years after her birth, Harris felt called to a life of service to Christ at a young age. She was very active in her church as a teenager, and later founded a young adults group at St. Barnabas Church in the Germantown section of Philadelphia.

After graduating from the Philadelphia High School for Girls, Harris immediately went to work. She joined Joseph V. Bakers, a black-owned public relations firm, and spent the next few years traveling around the country representing the firm's corporate clients. Harris later distinguished herself as a leader at the Sun Oil Company, where she headed the public relations department.

After her ordination to the priesthood, Harris served in a suburban Philadelphia parish. She received national attention as a columnist for The Witness *magazine, a publication that championed causes such as antinuclear activism; gay, lesbian, and women's rights; and environmental concerns.*

Harris' election as bishop in Massachusetts in 1989 sent shock waves through the Anglican Communion. Some of her critics claimed she lacked formal theological training, while others were wary of her progressive views. Harris was defended strongly by many, however, and remained characteristically tough during the controversy over her election. As she has said, "The temptation we all face is to play it safe; don't take risks; don't make waves. If Jesus had played it safe, we would not be safe, I would not be standing here today clothed in rochet and chimere and wearing a pectoral cross."

In the years following her consecration as bishop, many came to see her as one of the most important spiritual leaders of the latter half of the twentieth century, a force acting for change for women, people of color, and the poor around the world. She is widely admired for her courage, wit, intelligence, and forthright manner.

Following her retirement from the Diocese of Massachusetts in 2002, Harris accepted a call to serve as assisting bishop in the Diocese of Washington, D.C., beginning in the summer of 2003. She remains today what she has always been—an activist critic of the status quo who constantly strives to break new ground.

I was the third African American woman to be ordained a priest. Pauli Murray was, of course, first, and then Mary Atibonishau.

The earliest women ordained had a very rough time. It's much easier for women who are being ordained today. They don't know what some women went through regarding their ordination, call to ministry, and ability to function in parishes. Many could only be assistants in churches, or those assigned to their own churches got small churches that really couldn't afford pastors. The first eleven women and then the five who followed them in Washington, D.C., could find few places to celebrate communion, and the priests who did allow them to do this were sometimes disciplined by their own bishops. Those early days were very difficult for women. Women coming along today go through the process like men, with little or no difficulty. Their greatest burden is financial as they prepare for ordained ministry.

There are three dioceses in the Episcopal Church that still do not ordain women: the dioceses in Quincy, Illinois; Fort Worth, Texas; and San Joaquin, California. Ultimately the decision to ordain or not resides with that person's bishop. Although we have canons or church law that say the ordination process is open equally to men and women, and people want those canons to be enforced uniformly, the ultimate decision still resides with the bishop.

I would like women who feel called to ministry by their discernment, their community, to be able to participate openly in the ordination process, and not have to go some crazy backdoor route that one bishop has worked out so that women in his diocese can go to another diocese and be ordained.

I spent my first year as a deacon serving as an intern in the Church of the Advocate. Soon after my ordination, the bishop asked me to go to a small congregation just outside Philadelphia, and I was there from 1980 until 1984.

In 1984 I became the executive director of the Episcopal Church Publishing Company, which published *The Witness* magazine and also did a lot of programming. I wrote a column critical of the church, our government, and corporate America. The issues had to do with militarism, imperialism, capitalism, human and civil rights, the ordination of women, rights of gays and lesbians—that whole range of issues. People throughout the church didn't like things that I said, but there were a lot of people saying the same things that I was saying, both in print and by their actions. Having a column in a magazine is kind of like a pulpit, and I used that space to raise consciousness. It was an entity independent from the Episcopal Church. What could people do to me? The publishing company was not part of the Episcopal Church; that just happened to be its name.

I gave one of the addresses at a mid-'80s conference held at the Episcopal Divinity School in Cambridge Seminary to talk about women as bishops. "Let's face it," I said, used to speaking my mind, "we're talking about white women. They've got ten years in the priesthood. They've got the visibility." Following that conference, I was asked by a friend who was representing some women in a diocese of Massachusetts if I would allow my name to be put into the nomination process for bishop.

"Let me go pray about it," I replied, and about a month later I said, "Yeah, you can put my name in. I don't think it's going to go anyplace. But go ahead and put it in." At each step in the process I thought it would not go any further. Even as people came to Philadelphia to interview people I knew and to hear me preach, I thought it's not going to go further. I met with the whole nominating committee and said to myself, "This isn't going any further." Even as I was nominated on the slate of five people, I thought, "Not a chance." And I came to Massachusetts and met with people who were going to be in a series of meetings with voters in the election, and the thing that was uppermost in my mind was, "I'm never going to see these

Barbara Harris, age 17, high school yearbook photo

people again in my life, so I can say anything that is on my mind." Which is exactly what I did.

I kept pinching myself even up to the day of my consecration because I had trouble believing I could have been elected. A protracted process follows the election, during which the standing committees of a majority of dioceses in this country have to consent to the election. A majority of bishops have to consent to the election so that it becomes the will of the church. You are a bishop for the whole church, even though elected by a diocese. That consent process was touch and go, and ultimately, within the time frame specified, the required number of consents were received from both standing committees and bishops. The consecration could go forward.

Nobody can hate like Christians. Some of the mail that I got from church people was incredible, unbelievable. There were death threats, protests, objections at the consecration service itself. The Church of England to this day does not permit women bishops, and there were other provinces of the communion where bishops would not recognize my Ecclesiastical or Episcopal acts.

What surprised me was the vehemence with which some people expressed their beliefs. I didn't expect everybody to be pleased, but the mean-spirited things that some said and did were surprising. One diocesan newspaper ran my picture on the front page with a black slash across my face like a no-smoking ad. People raised all kinds of questions about my personal life and the fact that I was divorced. They said there had never been a person elected bishop who was already divorced, and divorced persons *have* been elected.

Because racism is so pervasive in the church, I'm sure that was a part of it. They had a lot of ammunition: I was a woman; I was black; I was divorced; I had not gone to seminary; I had only been ordained nine years; I was outspoken; I was left of center. Anything they wanted to use, they used.

But enough people were supportive and confident in my ability to exercise this office, and enough people were praying for me, that I felt supported. I was able to do what I was called to do.

At my consecration, a woman sat directly behind me who was a Boston Police Department detective. She was prepared to get me out of there had any violence broken out. The Boston Police Department had offered me a bulletproof vest to wear that day, which I declined. I thought, "If some idiot is going to shoot me, what better place to go than at an altar." I had some trepidation, but when I walked into that auditorium in procession and people greeted me so warmly, it fell away. I didn't know what was going to unfold in the service, in terms of the protests.

As I look back, a hallmark of my ministry was that I tried to pastor people and love the people of this diocese, especially people who had not felt cared for. I did not lose sight of the issues to which I had always been committed. I continued to testify at the statehouse against the reinstitution of the death penalty. I participated in demonstrations for issues that were important to me. As I preached and spoke to people, I always held before people the gospel imperative of justice.

There was a time when I said I would not talk to white people anymore about racism; I was tired of trying to educate white people. And God said, "You must continue to speak, that is your vocation. You cannot give up."

I would describe myself as feisty, passionate about loving and accepting people. My greatest regret is that things have not changed as quickly as I would like, but that's the history of the Church. Change is very slow. Racism is so institutionalized and so systemic in our society that it will not be eradicated unless people are intentional about its eradication; and until those who benefit the most from racism are willing to give up some of their power and privilege.

I advise youth to pursue your dreams and your aspirations with all the ability God has given you, and don't be deterred by criticism. Don't let people tell you your dream is pointless. Leaders don't wait for consensus, they make it.

Nobody can hate like Christians. Some of the mail that I got from church people was incredible, unbelievable. There were death threats, protests, objections at the consecration service itself.

—BARBARA HARRIS

CHARLES HARRIS

Born in Auburn, Alabama, on September 12, 1928

Educator, academic, college professor

Selected and interviewed by
NVLP Fellow Nadia Brown, Howard University

—◆—

Dr. Charles Harris retired from Howard University in 2002 after thirty-two years of service as a scholar, teacher, and mentor in the Department of Political Science. During his career he also served as a senior specialist at and chief of the government division of the Congressional Research Service. He was also associate director of the Executive Institutes, U.S. Civil Service Commission. At present he is continuing his research on D.C. government and politics, teaching a course at Howard, and serving as CEO of a family-owned mineral corporation.

In the winter my dad, with my help, cut cords of wood and we sold two horse-wagonloads of wood.

I was sent to Auburn by myself to deliver a load of wood. When I got to the white family's house that had ordered the wood, I couldn't get into the driveway to unload it because a car was there.

A black lady was working there as a cook. This lady knew us because we were one of the few families that had a car. We drove the car to school. She said, "Well, you can drive, don't you? I'll get Miss so-and-so's keys and you can move her car."

She got the keys to the car and gave them to me. But when I got in, I detected right away that this car was different. I didn't know what to do. I fiddled around with the clutch and with the accelerator, various other instruments, but it was different from ours. We had a Chevrolet. I don't know what that was, maybe a Studebaker or an Oldsmobile. But it was different. I finally just gave up.

I got out of the car and when I looked back, the car was slowly moving down the driveway, rolling down the driveway. Because I knew I had done something to take the brake off, I rushed back and managed to get in the car before it got to the street and stop it. Otherwise it would have crashed and would have done a lot of damage. But in doing so, I wedged the front door; more or less sprung it and disfigured the front door.

I told the cook about it, and she told the lady of the house, who came out, of course, to look at the damage. She was very angry when she came out. She looked at the door. There was not a lot of damage, but the door wouldn't close snugly anymore.

Finally she just looked at me and said, "I don't want your wood. Take your wagon and go on."

Here I was with this wagonload of wood. I was afraid to go back and tell my dad about it because he would fault me for tampering with the car in the first place. I didn't realize I should not have even tried to move her car. I'd caution young people [here] to know what you don't know.

I went around the block, pedaling that load of wood. Luckily I found another buyer for it and got the same amount of money for it. I never told my dad about that. He's gone, but he never knew about that.

I learned another life lesson one Easter. A lot of the ten-cent stores, Woolworth's and so forth, have a lot of decorated eggs left over. Well, I guess very few people buy Easter candy or Easter eggs after Easter.

Big boxes of candy eggs were donated to the high school to give to the black children. I was in the seventh or eighth grade and happened to be outside. The man who brought the eggs would throw a big handful on the ground, and the children would run and pick up the eggs to eat.

A teacher was concerned, and she asked him to let her have the eggs to distribute. He told her no, because he was having fun throwing them and seeing the children run at them like a bunch of chickens.

I looked at that and realized we were being treated like animals. But little children couldn't resist Easter eggs—red, blue, and green. He threw all of them on the ground, and they picked them up. That's how some things in life are passed out, and we have to consider if they're worth it if we have to be degraded to get them.

One last experience that taught me something worth passing on to youth: Opelika was the biggest city in Lee County at that time, the county seat. The courthouse was there, where all the government offices were located.

Well, in front of the courthouse—and it's still there today—is a long wall, right beside the sidewalk. This wall is about two and one half feet high, and it's a very comfortable place to sit, shaded by trees in the back of it. African American farmers, during my growing-up days, would come to town, and since it was segregated, there were no restaurants or cafes they could go into. They would sit on this courthouse wall and socialize. There were no telephones, no radios, no television at this time. You came to town to talk with people and find out what was going on. They would congregate on the wide sidewalk in front of the courthouse to converse about what had been going on during the week and to hear all the gossip. It was a very pleasant place. They would buy cold drinks, soda water, as it was called, and drink soda and talk.

The county elected a new sheriff and apparently he disliked seeing all these blacks congregated in front of the courthouse. This was the center of the city. One Saturday, when all the black people got to town, they found that syrup or oil had been poured on the entire length of the wall. Nobody could sit on it anymore. There were no places we could sit. Everything was segregated. This was the one place blacks had been able to sit down and rest for a few minutes when they came to town.

A prominent white lady whose family lived there in the city inadvertently brushed up against this wall and this oil got on her dress and ruined it. She was so upset about it that she went to the authorities and made them take off the oil. The next week that oil was gone.

This was an interesting twist of things——shows how being mean-spirited boomerangs.

JIMMY HEATH

Born in Philadelphia, Pennsylvania, on October 25, 1926

Jazz composer and arranger

———◆———

Jimmy Heath has long been recognized as a brilliant instrumentalist as well as a magnificent composer and arranger. Born in October 1926, Heath's musical genius first flourished in high school when he played alto sax. He later received his first touring job with the Nat Towles Band, based in Omaha, where he performed during 1945–46.

In 1948 Heath teamed up with his brother Percy, a bassist, and the two toured the United States and played at the first International Jazz Festival in Paris with Howard McGhee. During the following year Jimmy and John Coltrane joined Dizzy Gillespie for a two-year stay after which Jimmy and Percy joined with Miles Davis, J. J. Johnson, Milt Jackson, and Kenny Clark to form the Symphony Sid All Stars.

Heath played alto sax until 1951, when he switched to tenor sax. Wide recognition followed for his abilities as a tenor saxophonist, and for his compositions and arrangements. Heath's talents extended to the soprano sax and flute. Now a legend in his own right, he has composed and arranged music for such jazz greats as Art Blakey, Miles Davis, Dizzy Gillespie, Ray Charles, Cannonball Adderley, Clark Terry, Dexter Gordon, Ahmad Jamal, and Chet Baker.

Heath served as head of the jazz department at Queens College for eleven years. He has been nominated for three Grammy Awards and has received an honorary doctorate from Sojourner Douglas College in Baltimore. In 2002 Mr. Heath became the first jazz musician to receive an honorary doctorate in music from Juilliard. In January 2003 he received the American Jazz Masters Award from the National Endowment for the Arts.

My forte as a teacher is that I can communicate to young people, [and I have] a sense of humor, a sense of life, and know my trade and what I have accumulated from my peers over a long period of time. A person who went to school and got a doctorate but who has never belonged in the world of jazz cannot teach jazz, tell [students] about the experiences. I can't give them the experience, and I always bring out that you have to get out there and experience things and work. Jazz is hard work.

A jazz musician or improvising musician is a scientist. You are put to a test every time you get on the stage. Most of the times you can pass that test if you prepare yourself. Other times, you're gonna fail. But it's always daring. You have to have a confidence in yourself and about what you're doing. So you gotta work on it, what we call the woodshed, you gotta practice.

You need to listen to all kinds of music and absorb whatever you can from the music of the world. Now I'm listening to Debussy. I just got a chamber music CD of Debussy. Andre Watson plays on it. It's small group stuff, not the symphonies. I like to listen to it at night. I got my collection of classical music. If I listen to jazz at night, it keeps me too analytical. I'm wide awake.

Jimmy Heath, age 15, high school photo

I'm not striving for a Grammy. I've got a lot of awards. I play not for the awards, but for love. When I came up, I had no idea I would be as successful as I am. All I wanted to do was play better and go further. Music is a life's work—it continues; it never ends.

It's amazing what people have gotten out of twelve tones of the piano. Jazz is Afro American classical music. The maestro is Ellington; look how much music he made. "I want to be like him," I said as a youth. Role models are really what it's about. Duke Ellington is an icon for everybody. There are so many great composers out here—Billy Strayhorn, Kenny Durham. We had so many composers and arrangers of American music that never had any respect or got their due. To give this information to classes and say, "You've heard of Cole Porter and Jerome Kern and all those great writers. We still play their music. But there are others, romantic writers like Kenny Durham whom you haven't heard of," and I'll play something by him.

There are new ones too. Wynton [Marsalis] is writing very good now. He's carrying on the tradition, and I love him dearly.

Our history is a mystery. Somebody has to bring it out. And I hope to be doing so until the last day of my life. I'm going to teach what I found out about Afro American people and what we've contributed to the world. I'm always searching to find something new in music that I can present to the world. I know who the great people are. I respect those who went before me. I have a great admiration and respect for those who laid the groundwork for this music, and I'll never leave it. Music is what I'll do until I can't do anything else.

A leader has to be a leader by example and not just talk about being a leader. You have to do something and people will take notice. First you have to be exposed; people see what you can do. They'll figure out who's the leader up there.

My greatest achievement is survival; coming from a very poor family. I don't have to work anymore if I don't want to. I do this for pleasure now, for fun. I've taken care of my finances and I reached a point a lot of my colleagues never reached. They were just as talented; they were just unfortunate. I feel very fortunate. Sometimes, though, I regret not having been fortunate enough to go to music school and get degrees. I think it would have gotten me somewhere faster. I don't know if it would have gotten me to the same place I am, but it would have gotten me somewhere faster, quicker.

I would say to young African Americans, learn your history and value that. You must know where you've been to know where you're going, as my mentor, Dizzy, used to say. You have to have one foot in the past and one foot in the future.

The youth are victims of the media. They go buy what the media tells them—what to wear, listen to, go to. If you don't, you ain't hip. You have to be a person who searches on your own and finds out things for yourself.

If young African Americans study the history, they wouldn't say as some say to me, "Jazz is white people's music." That hurts. I grant you, there are white artists and the audience is white and Japanese. But when I was coming up, 60 percent of the audience was Afro American. Only 40 or 30 percent were white. How that turned around has changed the image, so that Afro American youths don't know that this music is a great achievement that our people suffered for. Louis Armstrong, one of our first ambassadors, suffered to chart a path for all of us jazz musicians. The guys who know the history of it know that.

I went on the Black College Network tour and I played at the Cosby Auditorium at Spelman and other schools—Jackson State, Florida A&M, South Carolina State and all. I was hurt that the black schools concentrated on marching bands for the football games and didn't pay enough attention to Afro American classical music. And I said so to some of the students. I know they didn't like it. I was hanging out at Tennessee State, where they had a two-hundred-piece band, and when we had the jazz class, only a few students came and half of them couldn't play as well in that idiom as some of the other schools I had visited—white schools in particular.

I said, "Y'all are practicing to be athletes, huh, 'cause you can throw your legs up and do all that. You got a hip march. You're gonna have to march straight to welfare if you're gonna try to play them instruments when you get out of here, unless you get serious about these instruments."

It's changed now. I was just at Howard and it's different now than when my buddy Bennie Golson went there. They have a great jazz program. It's looking up. The white schools have them; that's why some call it white people's music. In the last ten or fifteen years, it's become vogue to have a jazz program at your school. So it's getting better.

DOROTHY HEIGHT

Born in Richmond, Virginia, on March 24, 1912

Civil rights activist

———— ◆ ————

Legendary activist Dr. Dorothy Height has long been one of the country's most influential and effective leaders, working primarily to improve the lives of African American women. As the only woman among the so-called big six civil rights leaders, Dorothy Height has been a powerful advocate for racial, sexual, and economic equality.

Among her achievements, Height created the Black Family Reunion, an annual gathering of African American families around the country. As head of the National Council of Negro Women, she helped build the organization into a force representing an estimated 4 million African American women. Her countless awards and honorary degrees culminated in 1994 with her receipt of the nation's highest civilian honor, the Presidential Medal of Freedom.

Presidents from Ronald Reagan to Bill Clinton have sought her advice. Arts and entertainment icons from Bill Cosby to Maya Angelou call her a friend. African American women have looked to Dorothy Height for decades as their unwavering voice in the corridors of power.

In the course of my work with the Young Women's Christian Association in the later years of the Civil Rights Movement, I chose to call a conference of black women. Some black woman wondered why I was doing this, but the executive director had every confidence in me. She knew that I was not trying to pull people out; but was trying to see how black women who were members and leaders in the YWCA could make their maximum contribution. I also wanted to see how the YWCA responds to help fulfill these women's rights and determine what opportunities they should have. The conference of five hundred black women was held in 1970 in Houston, Texas, where the YWCA was meeting in the South for the first time since the '30s. By this time, we had passed desegregation legislation and new civil rights laws. And out of that meeting came one imperative: to thrust our collective power toward the elimination of racism, wherever it exists. That was a radical change. The way we went about it meant that a small consensus grew, and today, that imperative is a part of the YWCA's purpose for being. After almost thirty years now, it is central to the work it does. So you can bring about radical change.

I always remember John McMurray saying, "If you go blowing off by yourself, you may even lose your own direction."

You have to challenge yourself by saying, "Who am I and what am I trying to do? What are my goals? Who am I willing to join in coalition with?"

Each person must choose their own purpose for their life. I never tried to imitate anybody else. I just tried to do what I felt I could do, to put in the most I could. When you see me attacking anything, I may fail but I always go at it, hoping I can put the best that I can into it. And I do pray. You have to be prayerful!

Some feel that because you don't shoot off with your mouth, you're

Dorothy Height, New York, ca. 1931

timid, not aggressive. At an early age, I learned from a woman, Mira Lester, who came to see me when I was in the hospital after I had an automobile accident, to think and speak of other people as if they are present. The only hope is that other people see *you* that way, too. But I've never enjoyed gossip, even as a teenager in high school. People would say, "Don't tell Dorothy, 'cause you know she won't get into it." That's been true all my life. My mother was like that; we never heard my mother misspeaking mean things about anybody.

I find when I get too involved with the "he said, she said," I'm diminished. I feel less valued. You might see something a person does wrong, with which you disagree, but always have respect for them. The fact that you are respectful of them doesn't mean that you don't see the places where you differ or where you feel they are wrong.

My mother's influence was very real in my life. I'll never forget when I was in high school and I won the Western High School Impromptu Speech Contest. That meant I would represent my school in the state finals. Before I left home for Harrisburg, my mother said to me, "No matter what happens, hold yourself together." When I got there with my principal and teacher, both white, the hotel manager saw me, and he told them he could not let me stay there because I was colored. I knew I had to appear that evening in the contest and reminded myself of my mother's words, "Hold yourself together." My teacher almost began to cry, she was so upset; she had no idea such a thing would happen. So I said to her, "Don't worry, if there's a delicatessen, I can make myself a sandwich, and I can put my dress on at Community Hall." And I did. I went to the auditorium. I was nervous.

There were seventeen contestants and I pulled number seventeen. When my time came to draw my subject, I drew the Kellogg-Briand Peace Pact [a treaty among sixty nations, signed in August 1928, which called for the renunciation of war as an instrument of national policy].

In my speech I said that Briand believed that peace would not come unless it was through the hearts of men, and that we will have to think more about each other and how we make that happen. I said that two thousand years ago, the message of peace was brought by a messenger whose parents were turned away at the inn, like my teacher, my principal, and I were that night when we were not accepted at the hotel. So when peace comes, it won't be through any instrument. It will require people changing their hearts.

I won first place. There were three thousand people in that auditorium, though the janitor and I were the only two people of color anywhere to be seen. And I have often thought about that day, because I was resilient, and they treated me equally.

That was a key experience for me, my mother's warning, over and above hanging the dress she had just ironed on the backseat, "Hold yourself together," prepared me. Many times, even today, when I listen and get quiet, and people wonder why. And I'm saying, "Hold us all together."

Many women have the idea that *power* is a dirty word. Mrs. [Mary McLeod] Bethune always said the important thing about power is how you use it, and I think that's true. A lot of people want power *over* people rather than power *with* them. Power and authority are both hard to deal with. You have to learn how to use it. I like the way the British talk about power related to organizations; they call it the "chair," and whoever is in the chair at this moment has the power in this group.

I lived through nine of the decades of the last millennium. Coming up to ninety, I'm astonished to see what I have tried to do carried forward, improved upon, and strengthened.

Life changes every day. The world is changing so fast that we have to be able to determine what are the major battles and the minor skirmishes. You have to determine what is valuable and what is not so you know how to build and carry forward. It's a commitment to set things on a course, to keep that course, and fulfill the needs of that course.

I feel faith makes you optimistic about the future. I have faith in the future. So long as God shall let me live, I want to be working towards equality and justice, knowing that I may not see it all, but I know I can see it better than when I found it. When you come to the end, you have to think to yourself, "I may not have achieved it, but I certainly tried. I gave it the best that I had, and I would do it again."

Our lives are so full of high expectations and frustrations. When we got *Brown v. Board of Education,* nine to zero, we thought of segregation, "Well, now that's finished," but that was just the beginning of a new struggle to make that stand.

So much still stands there to be done. But if you don't believe it can change, if you don't believe that you can improve the quality of life, you really can't. When I hear people say, "This organization is never going to do anything because of so and so," it becomes impossible to move it, because they don't see the potential. They just see what's going on. They have to be able to look beyond that, to drive forward.

This is not a time for rugged individualism. You have to see who you can form a coalition or work with. A. Philip Randolph always said, "We're at the banquet table of nature. There are no reserved seats. You get what you can take and you take what you can hold. But you can't hold anything without power, and power comes from organization."

So many want to be a part of organizations for the wrong reasons; it gives them a sense of elitism. They need to get beneath the surface, and they turn that into service. Doing something for others and helping carry forward change produce more satisfaction out of life in the long run. I often say to young people who say, "I can't be bothered with those old women, or some other women," that I have to be grateful that in my life, I could sit at a table with Bethune and Charlotte Hawkins Brown and Mary Church Terrell. Even when I had nothing to say, I was learning something. The important thing is for us to keep that connection, to draw upon our past, not to feel above it or discard it. See what it has to offer, and how to draw upon what all of our ancestors have done. Then you have a sense of roots; you've got a sense of history.

You can do something significant only by being part of a collaborative, organized effort. It's not uniformity, but a kind of unity that makes it possible for us to make an impact.

—DOROTHY HEIGHT

GEOFFREY HOLDER

Born in Port of Spain, Trinidad, on August 1, 1930

Dancer, painter, choreographer, designer, actor, photographer, writer

— • —

An actor, painter, director, choreographer, and author, Geoffrey Holder has done it all in an award-winning career spanning six decades. He earned Tony Awards for Best Director and Best Costume Design for the Broadway hit The Wiz. *His paintings have been exhibited in museums around the world. As a dancer, he has performed with the Metropolitan Opera, and choreographed classics for the Alvin Ailey Dance Troupe and the Dance Theater of Harlem. As an actor, his credits include everything from* Waiting for Godot *to the James Bond film* Live and Let Die, *to being the "Uncola Man" of TV-commercial fame. His latest achievement, in collaboration with author Jen Dunning, is the magnificent art book* Geoffrey Holder: A Life in Theater, Dance, and Art.

I had an incredible father, a strong, wonderful, brave, godlike man, and an artistic mother. Everything my mother did became magic. She was a Gemini. She could sew and when she put on the clothes she made,

Mother was gorgeous. My oldest brother was Boscoe, and of course the first boy was the apple of Daddy's eye—his boy.

Daddy had dreams. We lived in a small, charming house, but Daddy bought an enormous piano. It was too big for the living room, but it was for his son. Boscoe played on the piano—pink, pang, tan-tan, tan-tan—and Daddy said, "Aha, that boy has talent!" He took what money he had and sent Boscoe to learn to play the piano. Boscoe came home and played Chopin—la-da-da, da-dee-da—the music filled the house. It was the best thing that could happen in the house.

Then Mother had another boy. Kenneth was a footballer, yet Daddy gave him a violin. So we had la-la-la and da-dee-da—more music in the house. Daddy loved it.

Then came two girls. Mazi was gorgeous; she looked like Father in drag. The same face, but gorgeous! My father looked like my sister—big, beautiful bone structure. Then Magri was next and then little Jean, my first dancing partner. I am the last.

The dances of my youth were the Lindy Hop, Susie Q, Boogie-Woogie, and Shim-Sham-Shimmy. I watched Boscoe dance, and what Boscoe did, I copied.

Jean and I used to dance the Lindy Hop in Boscoe's show. One day Boscoe threw me onstage, and I began to ad lib. The audience applauded, and my head got big. Bah! I believe in having a big head. Everybody, especially all young kids, should have a big head, because as you grow up, that head gets knocked down to size, to the right size. You have to have something to knock down.

It's the environment that makes a child, and the environment I grew up in was divine. Families stayed together. We all listened to the same radio program. Whether it was *The Shadow* or *The Inner Sanctum,* we all listened to it, and we all got scared together. Jean would hide under Mother and I would hide under Daddy. Today the daddy is looking at sports; the mama is looking at *Oprah;* the child is looking at MTV. They don't have conversations. They can't share. But we did. I chose my father and my mother because I had to be born into that family; they had to teach me something.

Our house was the center of the storm because Boscoe played the piano. The piano was equivalent to an electric guitar today, and he used to play for parties. All the beautiful girls and handsome boys came around.

Then Boscoe learned to draw. He asked Mother how to draw a face. Mother used to draw silhouettes—an egg with two slits, that's all. From there Boscoe had to learn on his own. Mother's father was a painter—I didn't know that until recently—so it was etched in the family, in our blood. He began to draw gorgeous Trinidadian girls and boys. Trinidad is so cosmopolitan; nobody is "black" in Trinidad; everybody has four or five bloods. They're black and Chinese, black and East Indian, black and Portuguese, black and French, black and Spanish—we're all intermarried. We fall in love; we have beautiful children. All the mixtures are there. We're not "You black, me white." It's not "versus," but, rather, it's a matter of choice. My mother was raised here in the States, and she liked my father because he was very black. My father adored my mother because she was honey-colored. It's a matter of choice: do you like a black dress or a white dress? It's not "This is a white girl and this is a black girl." It's a matter of your taste.

When we were a British island, the British loved to put one race against the other—the Chinese against the Indian, for example—but what kept us sane is Carnival. Every Carnival day, we all danced together in the street. We all shook our buns. We all had two days, two nights dancing and singing in the streets.

After Ash Wednesday, everybody went their way. The obstacles we had were class. Trinidad has a British colonial class structure: what school did you go to, and who's your mother? Just like Charles Dickens, but with black faces. Strange!

I went to Queens Royal College. It was very prestigious and expensive, but Daddy scrimped the pennies. I was a shy guy because I used to stammer. I couldn't speak. Geoffrey Holder couldn't speak. I could think faster than I could speak. And I was dyslexic. I didn't know the word until Ennis Cosby made it known. It's important to know the word because otherwise you grow up feeling that you are a dunce when you can't read, or not well. Numbers also played games with me; I didn't know that was part of my dyslexia.

But I am blessed. I took that and I used it. If you cannot speak, you listen. Writers listen. If you cannot speak, you look. I can see better than somebody who talks too much. They're not looking. I walk the streets and I see the most beautiful people, people who don't even know they're beautiful. Gorgeous people. Not Hollywood gorgeous, basic beauty. What's beautiful is kindness and an attitude of respect for people. I'm a curious man. I'm seventy-one going on fifteen. And every day I go out, I see something for the first time.

I learned to listen, and listen to my son. Adults must listen to their children, because children see things adults don't see. He will see totally different things than I do and tell me, "No, Daddy, that's wrong. This is . . ." And I say, "All right."

I never knew that I could say certain things, never knew I had a viewpoint until all these wonderful people—Bill Dufty, Carmen de Lavallade, Jack, Edward—became my friends. All add to Geoffrey Holder being

"Age twelve in my Queens Royal College uniform when I was young and cute."
— Geoffrey Holder

Geoffrey Holder. I chose the best people as friends to learn something from them. I am still a little boy, age fifteen. I'm still looking for knowledge.

I have a good friend from Saudi Arabia. I want to know about his religion. I want to know about everybody's religion so I can understand their mystery. But I'm not following anybody. I don't want anybody to follow me. I'm not going to stop anybody. I do things from my truth. All I can give you is my truth, whether you like it or not. When I look into a mirror, I see God. I may be in His image; He may have big lips just like me.

You know love late in your marriage. You know devotion and respect for each other. Real love comes late in your marriage. Likewise with friendship. The people who called me when the World Trade Center was hit from all over the world, those were friends who were concerned about me.

It's very important that you touch. I gave a lecture in North Carolina, and a boy said, "Mr. Holder, can I get a hug?" So I hug. The boys hugged me. Then the teachers came over and said, "Geoffrey, that is not done in this school. You're not supposed to touch the children."

Body language is very important. You can say so much with the body. It does not lie. You can tell a man by the way he walks. That sensitivity develops when you're dyslexic. You become very, very sensitive.

I also love old people, because old people become the historians. They'll say, "In the fifties, when I bought that hat, it only cost me five bucks. But when I wore the hat like this, it was lovely," or "We went to the ballroom up in Harlem and we danced."

They're all historians and should be highly respected.

Ask questions. You're not ignorant when you do so; you are wise. When you pray to God, don't say, "God, give me a new car." Say, "God, all I want is wisdom." Wisdom will get you through everything.

Find your great-aunt or your favorite godmother, and ask them questions. They'll give you all the answers—their way. They are the writers of the book. You don't have to read the book. Just talk to them.

All I can give you is my truth, whether you like it or not. When I look into a mirror, I see God. I may be in His image; He may have big lips just like me.

—GEOFFREY HOLDER

OLA G. HUDSON

Born in Nashville, Tennessee, on June 9, 1930

Educator

Selected and interviewed by
NVLP Fellow Shyretta McCrackin, Fisk University

———————

Even as a young child, Ola G. Hudson aspired to be an educator. In elementary school, she spent her hard-earned nickel not on bubblegum and lollipops but on attendance roll books for her next "pretend" class. In 1953 she stood before her first class of students at Natchez High School. She devoted forty years to the Nashville Public School System, where she taught and served as coordinator of Home Economics and interim director of Vocational, Adult, and Community Education. She has been a member of Alpha Kappa Alpha Sorority for more than fifty years, and was recently named the Golden Soror of the Southeastern Region of AKA. Hudson also serves as the president of the Metropolitan Nashville Retired Teachers Association and chairman of the trustee board of Spruce Street Baptist Church.

My dad worked all of his professional life at the Sunday School Publishing Board, which is a part of the National Baptist Convention, USA, Incorporated.

Most of us children were born either during or around the Depression years, and the last thing people paid for at that time was Sunday school literature. My dad was supposed to get paid every two weeks, but there were many Fridays when he didn't get paid. He had to do extra jobs in order to buy food for us to eat. The two chairs you see on my front porch were made by my dad, who died in 1962. He used his skill in carpentry to augment his paycheck, so that his nine children could have food to eat when the paycheck didn't come on schedule.

We were very, very poor, as far as money was concerned, but we were rich in those things that, I've learned later in life, are the most important. We had parents who were loving and concerned about us, although they were not so doting that they allowed us to do as we wanted. We had to study; we had to go to church; we had to play fairly with each other; we had to extend ourselves and use our talents in the community and in the church. I realize now that we were very, very rich.

We lived most of our growing-up years in rented property, none of which had the modern conveniences we now have. I lived in my first home with indoor plumbing and an indoor bathroom after I graduated from college. We weren't unusual, because in the black community, during the '30s and the '40s, and even into the early '50s, most people I knew lived the way we lived. But we laughed a lot, and we played a lot, and music was very important.

My dad graduated from Tuskegee. It was called Tuskegee Institute at that time. He was a member of the band, and playing an instrument was another way he supplemented his income. He actually taught music lessons to children and even adults.

My mom was a former choir member. We used to tell her she knew every hymn in the songbook. We sang a lot, and we had a good time. As each sibling grew older and got a job, they assisted the rest of us who came behind. I had what I thought was a normal childhood. While our resources materially were few, we were rich in those important intangibles.

I started going to Tennessee State, when, if I remember correctly, tuition was either $15 or $20 a quarter for those of us who were in-state students. I received a scholarship. When I graduated [from high school] I received a scholarship from Delta Sigma Theta Sorority for $100. That paid for a whole year. But one of my favorite teachers was an English teacher, and she wanted me to go to Fisk and major in English. My mother, a very wise woman who didn't talk a lot, helped me see that my strong suit was home economics, which was another area I liked and a subject [for which] one of my favorite teachers had strongly mentored me. My mother helped me see that I couldn't afford to go to Fisk, even though I had a scholarship for one year. So I ended up at Tennessee State, which was then called NI State College. It was very different from what it is now. Even though I've lived in Nashville all my life and watched it grow, I'm still amazed every time I go out and see the administration building right in the middle of what used to be Centennial Boulevard.

At the time I studied there, home economics was housed on the third floor of what I think is still called the Women's Building: it was the building where the main cafeteria was. It was much smaller then—during or right after the second World War.

There were a lot of barracks on the campus where veterans lived, and all of the sociology and psychology classes that I took were in what they called the GI buildings. Those were temporary barracklike buildings on the campus.

The cafeteria was the center of the life on campus. The environment was nurturing. Historically black colleges and universities still have that going— they're small enough that teachers know the students. Like our teachers in high school, our NI teachers knew that we didn't have all of the resources that other universities had, but they made up for the lack of resources in the things that they did for us, even if it involved using their own money.

Once I started teaching, I was glad that I [had gone] to a college that did not have all the modern conveniences, because we learned to be creative. We learned to use our own ingenuity or our own resources, and to take what we had and make what we wanted.

I never remember not wanting to teach. I remember telling my mother at a very early age that I was going all the way through school because I was going to be a teacher. One of the games that we used to play as children was "rock school." You'd put a rock in your hand and close your hand. The other person would have to choose the hand that held the rock. They would touch the hand they guessed it was in, and if it had the rock in it, they would be promoted to the next grade. If we didn't play rock school, we actually played school, with different ones of us assuming the role of teacher.

When I was in eighth grade, I went to the five-and-dime store and bought a roll book. I kept my roll as the teacher called the roll.

From my earliest childhood, I always wanted to be a teacher, and I can remember now almost every teacher I had, from first grade through elementary school through junior high school and even high school.

Now that I know what real teaching is, I know I had great teachers for the most part. I had excellent teachers.

ESTHER COOPER JACKSON

Born in Arlington, Virginia, on August 21, 1917

Editor

Selected and interviewed by
NVLP Fellow Jamie Walker, Howard University

———

Esther Cooper Jackson was one of three children born to Esther Irving Cooper and George Posea Cooper. Raised by an activist family, it is not surprising that Jackson took part in the Civil Rights Movement. She worked with the Southern Negro Youth Congress and was co-founder of Freedomways *magazine. She worked with such notable figures as W. E. B. DuBois, Shirley Graham DuBois, Paul Robeson, Ossie Davis, and Ruby Dee. Jackson has won a Lifetime Achievement Award from the New York Association of Black Journalists, the Rosenwald Fellowship, and was awarded an honorary doctorate from Long Island College.*

My parents always had discussions with us around the dinner table about segregation, struggles that were taking place, historic events, the heroes in our history. My mother, particularly, was very much aware of struggles taking place among African Americans all over the country. We always had the *Crisis* in our home and we always *read* it, especially Dr. DuBois's columns. Once a year, the *Crisis* would run pictures of children, and my oldest sister was pictured. This was a big event for our family.

My mother was involved in protesting the condition of black schools in Arlington. She organized delegations that went down to the state capitol in Richmond to protest the kind of materials and textbooks we were getting. My two sisters and I only went to Arlington schools for the early grades. Then my parents sent us to Washington, D.C., schools. We were delivered to our Uncle George Richardson's house on Sunday nights and spent the week with Uncle George and Aunt Ida. My dad picked us up at the end of the week, and we spent weekends with our parents. All of this was so that we could have better schools. We went to sixth, seventh, and eighth grades in the Washington schools, which were segregated but were some of the best schools that blacks had anywhere in the country. We got black history very early. Some of our teachers at Lovejoy School and at Dunbar High School in Washington were highly trained, highly educated, motivated.

When we went to high school, we came back home to Arlington and commuted because Virginians were permitted in high school to attend Washington, D.C., schools.

My greatest lesson was to always struggle, to fight for what we believe is right. My parents and teachers taught us that we had, as African Americans, a glorious and important history and to take great pride in who we are. We never felt we were the least bit inferior. We knew we came from a great people, a noble people. We learned this from the time we were small children throughout our lives.

Mother was a very dignified woman who held her head high. She would not let anyone call her by her first name: it had to be Mrs. Cooper. If some salesperson called her otherwise, she would correct them. She had nothing to do with them if they didn't address her properly. She was known in the community for this strength of character, and she passed this on to my two sisters and me. It helped us throughout our lives, as did the values held in our family. We had many books, even encyclopedias, and we had them before we had indoor toilets, before we had electricity. My parents were never keeping up with the Joneses, they had deep values.

My mother was active in the Baptist Church. She went to St. John's Baptist Church, which was on Columbia Pike in Arlington. It was one of her many activities. She couldn't have lived with my father, a nonchurchgoer, all of these years if church had been super important to her. We went to Sunday school. My dad would give us money to take to Sunday school, saying, "Your mother wants you to have this." We participated in the young Baptist program, reciting poetry and so forth.

My father was not religious at all. He was what we called the town atheist, except he was a Deist. He felt God was in nature, in trees and plants and the beauty of the world. I learned recently that Emerson was a Deist; Thomas Jefferson was a Deist. My dad used to say this is what he was.

So we had a combination of the two: Deist and Baptist. My father was a wonderful human being, and the fact that he was a nonbeliever had a big impact on my two sisters and me. When I worked in the South with the Southern Negro Youth Congress, I worked with many church groups, and attended church services, but it was never a major part of my life. I think it was his influence.

JOHN H. JOHNSON

Born in Arkansas City, Arkansas, on January 19, 1918

Publishing pioneer

———◆———

John H. Johnson is one of America's most successful and wealthiest entrepreneurs. Ebony *magazine, his flagship publication, is the nation's number one African American–focused magazine, with a monthly readership of more than 11 million. In 1982 he became the first African American to be named one of the four hundred richest people in America by* Forbes *magazine. In 1996 President Bill Clinton awarded him the Presidential Medal of Freedom, the highest civilian honor in the nation.*

As a young man, in 1936 he was offered a tuition scholarship by the University of Chicago, but Johnson had no way to pay for expenses. After impressing Harry Pace, president of Supreme Liberty Life Insurance Company, with a speech he delivered at an Urban League dinner, Pace offered Johnson a job as an office boy. This job provided him with the funds to attend college.

In little time, Johnson's abilities led to increased responsibility, and he eventually became Pace's personal assistant. One of Johnson's tasks was to collect news articles of interest to the black community and then brief Pace on them. It was at this point that the idea for a black news publication was born.

Unable to secure any bank financing for his project, Johnson created the Johnson Publishing Company with a $500 loan against his mother's furniture.

In November of 1942 he began publication of the Negro Digest. *It was a success from the start and with the help of magazine distributor Joseph Levy,* Negro Digest *circulation reached fifty thousand in only six months. During this time he also married his wife, Eunice.*

Trying to reach an even wider audience, Johnson modeled his next project on magazines like LIFE *and* Look *and created* Ebony, *a magazine designed to bring hope and positive images to African Americans following World War II. In addition to highlighting the achievements of successful African Americans,* Ebony *also dealt with the political and social issues facing blacks in America. The unparalleled success of the publication led ultimately to the creation of* Tan, Jet, Hue, Ebony Man, *and* Ebony Jr. *Johnson also expanded his media ventures into radio, television, and book publishing.*

Along with his innovations in media, Johnson is on the board of trustees for several major corporations and has received many important awards, among them the NAACP's coveted Spingarn Medal. In 1989 Mr. Johnson published his autobiography, Succeeding Against the Odds.

My father was killed in a sawmill accident when I was six years old, so I don't know a great deal about him. But I know a lot about my mother. My mother never went beyond the third grade because she worked on a farm. People picked cotton rather than go to school. I never had the feeling that she wasn't the smartest woman in the world.

I had a half-sister, but she was fourteen years older. So she was away most of the time. Her name was Beulah Lewis. I really didn't know her that well. Down south, in those days, if you finished high school, you could teach school. She had gone to another city, finished high school, and was teaching school. I was just like an only child.

We lived in a small town, population about 600. It was a riverboat town on the Mississippi River. The river was within walking distance of our little house. I was only nine years old, but I remember the 1927 flood very well. We were coming from church one Sunday afternoon and word came that the levee had broken some thirty miles away and everybody should run for the levee. We ran for the levee. No clothes. No money. No nothing. You couldn't even take your pets. We spent six weeks on the levee before the water went down. The Red Cross—I've always had a lot of respect for the Red Cross—came in seaplanes and brought blankets and tents and water and food. And it wasn't so bad!

All our homes were gone. I hoped we'd lose ours! It was a three-room house, a shotgun house, one you walked straight through. It had an out-house. There was no inside plumbing. The roof was tin. The rest was wood. The houses all floated away in water that was twenty feet deep, and the Red Cross would help you refurbish your house if you could find it; but if you couldn't find your house, they'd give you a new one.

I said a prayer every night that they wouldn't find my house! But they found it. Full of snakes and all the other things that crawl around rivers. They cleaned it up and moved it. That's when I first knew you can move houses. They moved it from wherever it was, so many blocks away, to our original location. I don't remember whether they found our outhouse. I doubt it. White people had toilets, but black people had outhouses.

There was only one black person who had a toilet, and he was a builder who built most of the white people's homes. He had a daughter, Willoughby.

We'd go to her house to play with her on Sundays and flush the toilet and wonder where the water went! By those standards he was wealthy because he had a toilet. And he had a car. I had to walk everywhere. No telephones either. The only telephone was in the grocery store. People would get messages from far away if someone died. They'd call the grocery store, and the grocery store would send an errand person over to your house and tell you what happened.

I had a good life. I didn't know there was a better life! There was a lot of prejudice and discrimination, but my mother kept me away from that. She said, "Son, don't do this and don't do that." So I never went anywhere to challenge the system. She worked for a white doctor and let me tag along to do errands to know where I was. We were known as Dr. McCampbell's "niggers," and nobody bothered us. He was considered our protector. It's something like the prison system: if you hang on to somebody bad, none of the other bad people will bother you.

He was a big, tall guy. There was a pharmacy downstairs from his office, and he sent me downstairs to pick up a prescription. The pharmacy staff didn't know what I was coming in for and said, "We don't serve any niggers in here."

I ran upstairs crying and told my mother, who told the doctor. He went downstairs and beat up the guy and said, "Don't ever call my niggers no nigger!"

I was a good student. The teachers in our segregated school made us good students. They were empowered to use the strap! And they would beat you up, tell your parents what they did, and your parents beat you up again. I was always under some kind of surveillance. It was actually a nurturing environment. School was not just the books. Your shoes had to be

John H. Johnson, early in his publishing career

shined. Your clothes had to be clean. You had to be respectful to your elders. It was a good system.

But it only went to the eighth grade. I've always thanked the Lord that it only went to the eighth grade because that caused me to come to Chicago, and that's why I happened to do as well as I've done.

My mother began to save money when I was in the sixth grade because she knew we'd have to go to Chicago. She had a friend there who told her that if she came to Chicago, we could stay with her until my mother could get a job.

Our goal was to get to Chicago so I could go to high school, because we knew I couldn't go away to school. [My mother] wanted me to be educated. I don't think she had the vision that I could go to college, but she wanted me to finish high school.

My mother and I moved to Chicago. My stepfather wouldn't come. He said there was cold weather in Chicago. There were gangsters. And he said, "The boy might not amount to anything anyway! Why should you make that kind of sacrifice?"

I've always had so much respect for my mother, because she truly loved him and she was a young woman at that time. But she was determined to defy him and everything else to get me a better education.

One day in July 1933, we boarded a train leaving Arkansas. My mother cried. My stepfather cried. I cried. But we left.

I remember it as if it was yesterday. The train came in at Twelfth Street, the Illinois Central Railroad. I'd never seen so many black people. I'd never seen so many tall buildings. I'd never seen so many cars. It was an awakening.

Life was difficult. At first my mother was able to get day work. She got paid by the day, plus carfare. This was during the Depression, now. The time came, about 1934, when she couldn't get any kind of job. After we didn't go back, my stepfather finally came. He was looking for a job as a street cleaner or anything, and he couldn't get a job. We went on welfare in 1934 and stayed on until 1936.

My mother was very sad about it, but there was no other choice. When we applied for welfare—they called it "relief" then—they said we hadn't lived in Chicago long enough, that we were not eligible. My mother wrote a letter to President Franklin Roosevelt. Somehow that letter got back to Illinois, and they put us on welfare. My mother always believed that Roosevelt personally read the letter and personally called up the people and made them put us on welfare!

Welfare in those days did not give you money. They gave you food. Big trucks would come into the community passing out supplies and food, and stop at your house. Other little boys and I would be sitting on a corner, and the truck would stop at my house. I'd say, "No, that's not my house. You know I don't live there!" The embarrassment! But that was a good thing; we wanted to get off welfare. Unfortunately, now, some people don't want to get off.

We got off when my stepfather got a WPA job. I was in high school and I got a National Youth Administration job. That was under Roosevelt's New Deal. It helped many of us. There was no other way to survive. It was a good thing.

In Arkansas there were no political parties for black people. When my mother got to Chicago, the lady we were living with was a Democrat, so we were Democrats. But we were for black elected officials. I remember going to a meeting over the Oscar DePriest vote. He was the first black congressman from the North. Up until then they had all been from the South.

The kids made fun of me because I had "mammy-made clothes," and I spoke with a strong Southern accent. All of them were from Chicago, so they used to poke fun at me. But it was the best thing that ever happened to me, because it made me determined to get back at them. The only way I could get back at them was to be smarter than they were.

I studied harder. I practiced public speaking in front of the mirror. When my junior class organized, I was the only one who had enough nerve to make a speech. They elected me president. I was president of the senior class, president of the student council, editor-in-chief for the school paper. I began to feel good about myself.

I never set out to get rich. I set out to do better than I was doing. I was making $25 a week at the insurance company. I was looking forward to making $100 a week. I set small goals because small goals can be achieved.

After you achieve a small goal, you have the confidence to go on to a bigger goal. You can't sit around waiting for someone to drop opportunity in your lap. You've got to go with what you have. You've got to start from where you are. That's what I've always done.

Always be honest about everything. My mother taught me that.

To this very day I don't smoke or drink. People ask me why. They think I am peculiar. When I was about eight or nine years old, my mother caught me and some other little boys in the backyard smoking corn shucks and drinking homebrew—there was no beer you could buy, so everybody made his own beer—and she gave me a licking I still remember!

Then she hugged and kissed me and said, "Son, this hurts me more than it hurts you."

I said okay. I dared not disagree with her. But I wasn't going to enthusiastically agree!

When I got old enough to drink or smoke, I never wanted to. It made an impression on me.

I have always been a great reader of black newspapers, and black newspapers have always had the job of getting rid of race prejudice, of calling to the attention of black people the mistreatments that are going on around the country and around the world. I got tired of reading about that all the time. I wanted to be happy some of the time! I wanted a magazine that would not try to do what they were doing—which they do exceedingly well—but a magazine that would deal with the positive things in life. I wanted a magazine that would deal with what people are proud of, with successes; so people in one city could see the success of people in another city, and would be inspired to do better in their own city. *Ebony* is a magazine devoted to making people feel good, making people proud of their heritage. The first time I ever saw a black person in print in a tuxedo, it was in *Ebony*. The first time I ever saw a black wedding was in *Ebony*. We have tried to cover some of the difficulties. We have the only pictures of Emmett Till in the casket. I remember years ago the *Jackson Daily News* called me and wanted to buy the photographs. I said, "No—you should've taken them when it happened!" I said, "Don't even offer me any money, because there is no amount of money you could give me that would make me do it. Because you should've done it when it happened." But at the end of the day, I say, "I want to feel good about myself."

Leadership means you've got to be the best at whatever you are doing. You can't just tell other people what to do; you've got to do it yourself. Give every job all you have. Be willing to tackle difficult tasks.

I have great faith in the future. Black people are better qualified now. We are also more courageous. More willing to fight for what we want. We will continue to make progress because we have a whole new group of well-educated people who are working in major corporations and starting their own companies.

Howard Owen Jones

Born in Cleveland, Ohio, on April 12, 1921

Radio evangelist, educator

Selected and interviewed by
NVLP Fellow Imani Miller, Oberlin College

———•———

Dr. Howard Owen Jones served as the first African American associate evangelist of the Billy Graham team from 1957 to 1963. He was also the first black evangelist to conduct crusades in Africa and for several years served as a visiting professor of evangelism at Crown College in St. Bonifacius, Minnesota. He was the first African American broadcaster to be inducted into the National Religious Broadcasters Hall of Fame, which later honored him with the Milestone Award for fifty years of broadcasting. In 2003 Jones published his autobiography, Gospel Trailblazer: An African-American Preacher's Historic Journey Across Racial Lines, *written with Edward Gilbreath and with a foreword by Billy Graham (Moody Publishers).*

He presently lives in Oberlin, Ohio. His beloved wife, Wanda, passed away in 2001. Jones has five children and eight grandchildren.

I was working on the air in Cleveland and heard about a radio station, ELWA, in Liberia, that wanted tapes of Negro spirituals recorded by black churches. My wife, Wanda, and I were invited to Liberia, Ghana, and Nigeria for a series of evangelist meetings. We spent three and a half months in Africa. The Africans really rallied around our program, because they heard that Howard Jones was a black preacher from Cleveland, and they'd never heard of a black preacher on the radio.

It was very gratifying, and Wanda and I could not get over the reception we got. I mean, the people turned out! Signs all over the place. I'd never seen anything like this before. Taxicabs and buses were carrying my name. When we walked down the street, people would just come and gather around us. They said, "You're the first—we've never seen an American Negro before. We see white missionaries, but we never see black missionaries." It was like that in Ghana and Nigeria too. They constantly told me, "Howard Jones, we hear that in the United States you have great big black churches, powerful preachers, and great choirs. Is that right?" I said yes. "Then why is it that no blacks come to Africa to be missionaries? Why is it that the white missionaries always come?"

That was the question we got as we traveled across Africa, and it is the question that I like to deal with today. I believe that African American churches have a responsibility, and we need missionaries, we need doctors, we need teachers and Christian educators that can go to Africa and other Third World nations like the whites are doing.

The church today is the one institution that has the real answer. Unfortunately, many of our African American churches are weak at the level of the pulpit.

Kids go to grade school, high school, then they go on to college. Their professors and teachers have gone to school. They have prepared. They know where they're going. And the kid has to do his homework.

When young people come to some of our African American churches, they relate to the music, but when it comes to the message, they're lost because some pastors don't have a prepared text, they don't know how to "expound the word of God." They're not feeding the people the Word. They shout, they get emotional, they hoot and holler. But the young person there is lost, and he'll either stay out of church completely or find another church, where not only his emotional needs are met, but his intellectual ones.

Today we need more trained ministers, ones who are trained in the word of God. We need expository preaching. We need preachers who hold up a Bible and don't just take a text and then don't focus their sermons on it. Jesus went into the temple, opened the book of Isaiah, and talked. Then he closed it.

Young people want that. In our crusades—and I was with Billy Graham for thirty-five years—we ministered to thousands of people. I saw a lot of young people in my crusades, like in Billy's, but of course his [were] larger. Young people do come, even now.

I went to Cincinnati to be with Billy in a big crusade, and on youth night, we saw thousands of young people of all ages, all races.

The church of tomorrow must be a church that is really spiritual and has a message that's relevant—a message of hope, encouragement. That church must tell frightened teenagers that you don't have to be afraid, there is a Christ who can be with you. It must also have a message about the home—responsibility of marriage and family. The church needs to point out the heritage and hope in the black family in America.

DEL JUPITER

Born in Pensacola, Florida, on April 29, 1924

Librarian, photographer

Selected and interviewed by
NVLP Fellow Brandi Lee, Spelman College

—◆—

Del Jupiter worked as a school librarian for almost four decades. After she re-
tired from the Atlanta Public School System, she began conducting research
on her family dating back to 1750. Based on her work, she published three ar-
ticles in the National Genealogical Society (NGS) Quarterly. *One of those*
articles was chosen for the NGS Quarterly Award for Excellence.

She and her late husband, Ernest, were married for nineteen years.

I read. That's how we kept busy. We had public libraries that we could
go to, but my mother would buy us books at our birthday and Christmas, and we would swap books with our friends.

My fondest childhood memory is our picnics in the summer. When school
was out, we always looked forward to the picnics. My father worked for a mil-
lionaire who had an estate that overlooked a bayou. Public parks weren't good

for blacks in those days, so that was our private park. The Yankees came down for spring training about two weeks out of the year, so the rest of the year we had the run of the place. It was about forty acres and very beautiful.

At the picnics, we went swimming. We always packed a lunch. And Fourth of July and Labor Day, Daddy would get up early and go fishing. He'd catch all this fish and bring it back, and they'd fry fish outdoors in a bucket of charcoal with a big skillet on top. Mother made homemade ice cream and potato salad.

The girls would go swimming and then the boys would go. Girls and boys didn't swim together. My mother was strict and old-fashioned.

I was a biology major in college, and I went to grad school. I was working on a thesis project when I met my husband, and we were so busy courting, I didn't finish it. We married, and when my first child was born, I got a letter from a friend in California who was a children's librarian. My husband read the letter and said, "That's a good field for you to go into."

I did and I'm glad, because he was a minister and we moved around. The town always had biology teachers, but they always needed a librarian. I didn't have any difficulty getting jobs. And my biology background always helped me because when the high school kids would come in, I could always help them with their science.

My husband finished college at Baker College in Louisiana, went into the service, and came back to Atlanta University. The day we met, I was leaving the science lab, and it was raining. I was outside trying to get my umbrella up, and he said, "Well, ma'am, I could help you."

I felt as if I had known him all my life as he walked me to the dormitory. That night I was back at the science building doing some lab work. As I was leaving, I heard this fellow come up behind me and start talking. "You don't remember me?" he said. "The umbrella episode?" He walked me to the dormitory again that night, and we stayed outside and talked a long time. I got married on Christmas Day at home in my parents' church, the church that they married in.

I started photography before I retired from the library field. I had always had an interest, and I had always had a 35-millimeter camera. I decided to go to photography school. They were adult education classes that weren't expensive. One led to another, and then I took darkroom lessons. I had my own darkroom for a while.

Now I'm into genealogy. The skills I learned in photography were useful for me when I went around taking pictures of old sites and my relatives.

I had heard all of these stories when I was a child growing up about our roots in Pensacola at the time of the Spanish and pirates. In 1961, while my mother was visiting us in Houston, I said, "Mother, you need to put all these stories down. Because when you are gone, we won't know a thing." When she got home, she wrote a lovely story and sent it back to me. She went back five generations on her side and my father's side. I could get back to great-great-grandparents. But it was all tradition. I put it aside.

In 1968 I was here at Atlanta University taking a class in education under Dr. Horace Mann Bond. He told us many blacks didn't know their history and family history, and our assignment that year was to compile one. I learned about using the census records and the courthouse records. And I did that and put that paper aside. I thought that was a genealogy.

After I retired, I went to the public library, looking for something to read. I saw the book *Somerset Homecoming* by Dorothy Spruill Redford, in which she told how she researched her family history. She had a homecoming at the end of it on the old plantation where her ancestors had worked.

When I finished her book, I said, "Oh, I think I can do that." And I pulled Mother's story out of the dresser drawer. My greatest achievement was when I finished my family history.

I don't wear my religion on my sleeve. I say I'm spiritual inside. And I believe in doing what's right. You hear so much about people killing or stealing. Sometimes I think the perpetrators didn't go to Sunday school enough as children and learn the Ten Commandments. If you went to Sunday school and learned the Ten Commandments, you wouldn't do wrong.

DOLORES KENDRICK

Born in Washington, D.C., on September 7, 1927

Poet, educator

Selected and interviewed by
NVLP Fellow Adrienne Bailey, Howard University

———◆———

A native of Washington, D.C., Dolores Kendrick was appointed poet laureate of the District of Columbia on May 14, 1999. Kendrick is the author of the award-winning poetry book The Women of Plums: Poems in the Voices of Slave Women, *published in 1989. In 1996 a CD of music inspired by* The Women of Plums *was released, and Kendrick adapted the book for theatrical performance in Cleveland, Ohio, and at the Kennedy Center in Washington, D.C. The adaptation won the New York Professional Award in Theatre.*

She was the first Vira I. Heinz Professor Emerita at Phillips Exeter Academy, and one of the first original designers and teachers at the School Without Walls in Washington, D.C. Kendrick presently works with the D.C. Commission on the Arts and Humanities.

I grew up in the segregated historical LeDroit Park area. We had an extended family; my family knew everybody else's family in that area. We had a good living and placed value on our lives, and had great dignity.

I wasn't aware that people like Paul Laurence Dunbar had once lived in our neighborhood, people who made tremendous cultural contributions. Frank Snowden was at Howard University, and my mother and father associated with Sterling Brown. Then, I didn't know who Sterling Brown was. I just knew he was a great friend of my father's and they played tennis together.

As a child in Washington, a segregated city, I could not go to the local theaters because I was black; I couldn't go downtown because I was African American. I knew that if I went downtown to eat, I couldn't get into the restaurants; and even at the lunch counters, I would have to stand in the part segregated for blacks. To keep us from experiencing that racism, our families would feed us lunch before we went downtown, so we didn't have to take those indignities. They shielded us from those indignities in many, many ways.

My family did an amazing thing when I was growing up. They never sat down and pushed me to see this as a negative way of life that I would have to fight all of my life. They taught me, first of all, to be whatever profession I chose, but I had to be twice as good as the white person, twice as much was expected of me, and I had to be very good at what I did. Never start something you don't finish. Never make excuses. Stand up for what you believe, and be as honest as you can possibly be in your way of life. They also taught me to value myself as an individual.

The school system was so superb. The best school system Washington, D.C., has ever had was under segregation. There were the three schools—Dunbar, Cardozo, and Armstrong. We had wonderful teachers. The teachers would get the best out of you: they would never let you get away with doing anything halfway. These teachers demanded the best, the best education there was. Dunbar, at one point, was described as the Phillips Exeter Academy of Washington, D.C.

I didn't grow up with any sense of myself as less than anybody else there. I was aware of it, but I did not let it consume me, I did not let it own me. We were taught, if you let these things own you, you are giving them more importance than they really deserve. We had to own our own lives, own ourselves.

We had a happy life. We had a community of people whom we enjoyed. My brother had his friends. It was such a strong community. When we came home in the evening, the neighbors were sitting on their porches, usually the older people. As I went down the street, I had to say, "Good afternoon, Ms. Jones. Good afternoon, Ms. Brown," right straight through. When I got home, if I had missed one, my mother would say, "You didn't speak to Ms. Green."

After my father and mother divorced, she was a single parent, but that's a recent term. Black women have been doing that since slavery, and they've managed to raise strong families.

My dad was a businessman, and he got into business because of racism. He had a very good government job, as some black men did in Washington, D.C. The best jobs black men could get were with the post office or some government agencies. When his boss retired, another white man came in and called him a nigger and told him, "You have more, you're doing more than we allow you to do. You've got more power than we want you to have." I don't know if he used the word "power," but that was the import of it.

My dad walked right out of the job, right then and there. "You can have the job. You cannot have me, but you can have the job," he said. He was a young man with a family. He began to think of starting his own newspaper, and got a job with a paper that already existed in Washington called *The Gailey News.* My father was a great salesman. He knew how to sell, sell ads; he got around town. He took that talent and became his own independent person.

All of us achieved in spite of racism. [As a child], I had imagination. I would write stories in school. I was so happy creating stories. I just loved to write. It made me happy to let my imagination go to all of these various and sundry places, and to conceive of things, and to make things happen in the corners of my mind, and to put it down on paper. I didn't start writing poetry until I got into high school and one of my teachers had read my prose and told me that it was flowery, and that I had to cut away the fat of it. And with that I thought, well, why don't I try poetry, because I know poetry demands an economy of language.

[In *Through the Ceiling,* Ms. Kendrick's first book of poetry, published in 1975], I was thinking of a quote from scripture. A woman was dying, and they called for Christ; they sent for him, and they couldn't get her in the room in a normal way. She was on what we would call a gurney today, and she had to be carried in. So they decided to bring her in through the ceiling. They took her up to the top of the house, and they lowered her down through the ceiling to come to Christ, and Christ was waiting for her. To me, that had a very incredible import.

If in life we could have that kind of vision, if in life we could have that kind of strength to realize that Christ can come, he will wait for you if you have to come down through the ceiling. People will bring him to you, and he'll be waiting for you. But coming down through the ceiling and having the pain is part of your living.

You have to be sure you've got talent. You have to be sure writing is something you want to do above everything else. You have to be immune to rejection slips. Don't think becoming a poet is an overnight sensation. There are lots of venues that will make you think that, lots that will put you on a platform and make you think that you're a poet, when really you are in the infant stage of your art, if it *is* an art, and that you have to determine for yourself.

If you want to be published more than anything else, you're not really going to be a good poet. You need to write and write and write and write and write, and continue to do that, and perfect the art as you go along. Perfect!

Never start something you don't finish. Never make excuses. Stand up for what you believe, and be as honest as you can possibly be in your way of life.

—DOLORES KENDRICK

CORETTA SCOTT KING

Born in Marion, Alabama, on April 27, 1927

Civil rights leader

━━◆━━

Coretta Scott King, one of the most influential women leaders in the United States today, entered the world stage in 1955 as wife of the Rev. Dr. Martin Luther King Jr. Following his death, she continued his work as a leading participant in the Civil Rights Movement.

King grew up part of a poor, hardworking family in rural Alabama. She graduated as valedictorian from her high school, and went on to get a B.A. in music and education from Antioch College in Yellow Springs, Ohio. She then studied concert singing at Boston's New England Conservatory of Music, where she earned a degree in voice and violin. While in Boston, she met Martin Luther King Jr., whom she married on June 18, 1953.

During Dr. King's career, Mrs. King devoted most of her time to raising their four children: Yolanda Denise (1955), Martin Luther III (1957), Dexter Scott (1961), and Bernice Albertine (1963). In addition to raising her family, she dedicated herself to movement work, speaking before church, civic, college, fraternal, and peace groups.

Since her husband's assassination in 1968, Mrs. King has given much of her energy and attention to developing programs and building the Atlanta-based Martin Luther King Jr. Center for Nonviolent Social Change as a living memorial to her husband's life and dream. She has carried the message of non-violence throughout the world, leading goodwill missions to many countries in Africa, Latin America, Europe, and Asia. She was also the first woman to deliver the Class Day Address at Harvard and the first woman to preach at a statutory service at St. Paul's Cathedral in London.

Mrs. King has held dialogues with heads of state as well as spiritual leaders, including Pope John Paul, the Dalai Lama, and Bishop Desmond Tutu. She has also distinguished herself as a remarkable organizer, bringing together eight hundred human rights organizations to form the Coalition of Conscience in 1983.

One of the most celebrated African American leaders of our time, she has received honorary doctorates from more than forty colleges and universities and has written three books and a nationally syndicated column. She has served on and helped found dozens of organizations, including the Black Leadership Forum, the National Black Coalition for Voter Participation, and the Black Leadership Roundtable.

A woman of wisdom, compassion, and vision, Coretta Scott King has tried to make ours a better world and, in the process, has made history.

I was a tomboy growing up. I could climb trees. I could wrestle with boys, and I did. I used to fight my sister and my brother when they did anything that I didn't like. So they used to call me mean. I thought, "My goodness, I don't want to be mean." But for a long time, I thought that I was going to be.

Coretta Scott King at age 12

They would say, "You're going to the devil. That's what's going to hap-pen to you because you're so mean. And then you're not going to have any friends. Nobody's going to like you."

Thinking about all of that, by the time I became a teenager, I began to be much more ladylike. I stopped fighting. By the time I went away to college, I was quite the young lady.

My siblings and I tease about the fact that I became involved with a nonviolent movement!

Later, when my children came, my husband said, "You don't have to whip them. I think you can just talk to them." I tried it. I talked and I talked, and I found that sometimes you had to do a little more than talking! One day I left him with the kids, and he found out that *he* had to do a little bit more than talk to them!

I did not go to college to find a husband. That never occurred to me. I certainly wanted to be married, but I had a career ahead of me. And I needed to get as much of that done [as possible] before I thought about marriage. I had boyfriends. But I was not interested in getting married until I got my education, because that was the most important thing to me.

I kept hearing about this young man, M.L. King Jr., a brilliant young man who was working on his Ph.D. And he's an excellent speaker. And he's going to be very successful, he's a preacher, he's a minister. And, no, I'm not interested. So I just dismissed it.

I had this stereotype in my mind of what preachers were like—overly pious and not very interesting. I wanted to meet someone who was exciting, and I didn't want to be a minister's wife and subject my family to living in a parsonage. I just didn't want that kind of a life.

Our first contact was by telephone. He says, "This is M.L. King Junior. A mutual friend told me about you and said some very wonderful things about you. And I want to get to know you. I'm here at Boston University, studying for my doctorate in systematic theology." So I said, "Well, I'm here at the New England Conservatory of Music."

He said that he was like Napoleon, and every Napoleon has his Waterloo. "You are my Waterloo, and I'm on my knees. All the things I heard about you make me want to meet you. And now that I've talked with you, I really want to meet you. When can I see you?" I said, "Well, I have time on Thursday between classes for lunch." He said, "I will meet you at the Conservatory. It usually takes me ten minutes to get from Boston University to the Conservatory, but I'll make it in seven." He told me what car he was going to be driving, a '51 green Chevrolet. When I saw the car coming, I walked down and I saw him in the car. He was so short. He was very clean-shaven and looked just like a little boy. I had thought that I was going to meet a man! I was disappointed. But when he talked, his voice was very big, and he just made you feel so good. Martin had a way of making everyone feel special.

We went to a local restaurant, and during lunch he wanted to test me, to see whether or not I was a thinker, because he always placed a great value on thinking. The conversation had something to do with communism versus capitalism, and I made an intelligent comment. He said, "I see you know something other than music." And I thought to myself, "Of course I do, I've been to Antioch College."

On the way back to the Conservatory, all of a sudden he said, "You have everything I've ever wanted in a wife: intelligence, personality, character, and beauty. I want to see you again." I said, "I don't see how you can know this. You don't even know me." He said, "Oh, yes, but I can tell, and I'm serious."

From that point on, he continued to pursue his wanting to get married. "I'm very serious," he said. "When I finish my two years' residence, I will pass through a church in the South and I need the right kind of wife. I know what I want." He talked about his determination to fight to make changes because of the inequities in our society. He said, "I plan to do it from a Baptist church pulpit, because that's the freest place in the South." He seemed so sure that he was going to be able to do it.

So here I am, this early, having to decide whether or not I'm going to have a serious relationship. In the first place, you have to do the courting before you can get married, and if you find out that this is not what you want, you don't go forward with it. I was very clear about what I wanted to do in my life, and I wasn't going to let anybody stop me. But this young man was so persistent and determined, I knew I had to stop seeing him, because I would have fallen in love, and once you're in love, you can't really control the emotions. Too many people had invested in me, and I had invested and believed in myself. This was the most important decision that I would make in my life, and I knew that. So I prayed about it.

I tried to think of how it would be if, at a certain point in my life, I didn't have a family, didn't have love in my life. And I thought I would not be fulfilled if I only had my concert singing career. So I decided if God directs me to open my life to this relationship, then I'll follow wherever it leads, and that will be what I'm supposed to do. And that's exactly what happened. I stopped fighting, and we went on with our courtship.

I was a helpmate from the very beginning. And that's the kind of wife Martin wanted—somebody who could be a sounding board for his ideas.

The Montgomery bus boycott prepared me for what was to come. I had so many things to do, so many different roles I had to play. Our house was the center of activity in the beginning. We had to create an organization from a spontaneous movement. It wasn't easy, but it was exciting. It was exciting when the people stood up, fifty thousand strong, to boycott the buses.

I didn't know how dangerous it was initially until we started getting threats. But I thought many times they were empty threats. When a sheriff called and said to my husband, "If you don't stop and get out of town in three days, we're going to bomb your house and kill your wife and baby," I thought, "Nobody's going to bomb the house." But when the bomb actually hit, I realized we could have been hurt, we could have even been killed. My parents were trying to pull me away, and his parents were trying to pull him away. I had come to a peace within myself that I was not going to go anywhere. I thought, "I'm going to be right here, because this is right; this is what we are called to do."

Every time Martin went to jail, I went with him spiritually. I didn't ever go to jail during the Civil Rights Movement, which I regretted. He always wanted me to stay out of jail because of the children.

I did a lot of marches and so forth. I had been in the peace marches and the antiwar demonstrations that were being held throughout the '60s. There was a terrific price when Martin also spoke out [against the Vietnam War]. He was attacked by black leadership and white leadership to the extent that the coffers of SCLC started drying up. He said to me, "Coretta, you will have to make an appeal to your peace friends to make contributions to our organization." And of course I did. We got some funds. But we, the organization, not only suffered; personally it was very painful for him.

When I got word that Martin had been shot, I was shocked, but at the same time, it was like the call I had always been waiting for. So many times

I thought he was going to be killed. I never knew when. It's like a Greek tragedy. We know how it's going to end, but we don't know when, and we don't know where. I tried to prepare myself as best one can be prepared. You're never prepared. But I knew that Martin had lived so well, had made the ultimate sacrifice, and that his spirit would live on. That was my consolation. I wanted to see that happen.

I started praying for direction again after my husband's death. It just so happened that the King Center eventually became that direction. My commitment was to peace, freedom, and justice, to continue to make sure that Martin's dream was realized, that nonviolence became a part of our society. We're still moving in that direction.

Certainly it was not easy in terms of the way people saw me. I became a threat to some people who were around Martin; [there was concern] that I might be trying to take away from what they were trying to do. I felt that there had to be a place where people would come to learn about Martin, to study his philosophy, and his strategies of nonviolence. It was particularly important that young people understood what it was that the movement did, especially the nonviolent movement. If they understood that method, then they could use it in any situation they found themselves in. So I was determined to do what it was that God called me to do.

I think a lot of resistance came because I was a woman, and a woman is not supposed to do certain things. I've seen changes, but there's still a lot of work to be done in terms of people seeing women as being capable human beings.

A leader is a person who has character and a purpose. That purpose has to be something that transcends one's own particular interest, something that benefits the whole of humanity. I don't think a leader is always some-one who is identified by the media as a leader. There are leaders who are not visible, and they are making a difference. They are inspiring other people as well. Sometimes people mistake charisma for leadership. A leader has to have a vision, and has to be able to implement it.

LEATRICE MCKISSACK

Born in Keytesville, Missouri, on July 27, 1930

Businesswoman

———

Leatrice Buchanan McKissack is the chief executive officer of McKissack & McKissack Architects & Engineers, Inc., the oldest African American architectural firm in the United States. The firm is based in Nashville, Tennessee.

McKissack was literally raised on the campus of Fisk University, where her stepfather was dean. She later entered Fisk and earned bachelor's and master's degrees and became a teacher. She married William DeBerry McKissack, whose father was a Nashville architect and founder of McKissack & McKissack. When her husband died, she stepped in to lead the company. Despite her lack of business or architectural training in a traditionally male-dominated field, McKissack took the firm to new levels of success. Today her daughter Cheryl runs the Philadelphia and New York offices of McKissack & McKissack; and her twin sister, Deryl, runs the firm's Washington, D.C., and Chicago offices.

Mrs. McKissack has received local, state, and national awards, among them the Business Woman of the Year Award from the Tennessee Department of Economic and Community Development, an NAACP award recognizing her more than fifty successful years in business, and the Human Relations

Award from the National Conference of Christians and Jews. In 1990, President George Bush Sr. presented her with the National Female Entrepreneur Award.

I've always been one of those people who wanted to help the world. That's why I took on my husband's business—not for me, because I'm not an architect—I took it on for my girls, to hold on to the company until they were old enough to take it on.

Luckily I managed to survive that. Two years ago my daughter called and she said, "Mama, how're you doing?"

I said, "Oh, I'm okay."

She said, "Okay? What's wrong?"

I said, "Well, you know, I'm sick and tired of these architects and engineers squabbling amongst each other." I had an office in Memphis, one in Montgomery, Alabama, and I'm running up and down the road by myself, even on weekends.

She said, "What do you mean?"

"Well, my architect in the Montgomery office is fighting with our engineer here in the Nashville office. I'm so old, I don't want to be bothered with it. I just want all harmony. But that is not business."

"Mom," she said, "do you know how to spell the word 'over'? Pack your briefcase and go home."

I danced out of that office. I never, ever thought I would get to the point where I was tired of the business, because you get accustomed to that pace. Some people can't give it up. I gave it up easily.

I said to myself, "Okay, you've done this. Enough." When I taught school and became ill, I had to give up teaching. I just closed that chapter in my book. It was the same with the business.

The best days of my life—no bones about it—were when I was a housewife or homemaker, whatever you want to call us. All I had to do was make my husband's life happy, which I did, and care for my children. I enjoyed every day. Every day to me was like a blessed holiday.

When I married into the McKissack family, the first thing my mother said to me was, "Lea, you need to go back to school and get your degree in architecture."

"Mom," I said, "why would I ever want to do that? He does not want me in the business." And he didn't.

She said, "It's something you ought to do."

Do you know how many times I've thought about that? Instead of a master's in psychology, I should have been getting a master's in architecture. But when I married him, he did not want his wife to be an architect. He was proud of the fact that I had a master's, but still he was proud of me as a housewife, homemaker.

When my girls came along, it was totally different. Their father told them, "You can go anywhere in the world you want for college, but I'm only paying for one place: that's Howard University." That's where he went. "And you will be an architect or an engineer; you will be one of those two things."

When I finished college, I started off teaching. My father and my mother always guided me, and they said, "We didn't send you to college to sit at home. You need to make your own life, your own way."

It was not a major conflict in my marriage, but it was a challenging situation. My husband was a very gentle-spirited person. He did not like confrontation. So when I wanted something, I would just throw a fit, and everything would be all right. "Now Lea," he'd say, "I didn't need you to get upset." I would say, "I'm really upset. This is what I'm going to do. I'm going to teach school."

When I became ill, he was excited that I came home. I can't tell you how happy the man was when I [retired from teaching, and] came home.

But when he became ill, it closed a chapter in his life. I never thought he would accept me sitting in his chair in his office.

For three months, I went to the hospital every day. One day I said to him, "That's it. I cannot come in this hospital door another day. I'm taking you home today." He was so excited. I helped him get dressed, but I didn't take him home. I took him straight to the office.

He looked at that chair as if to say, "I don't know why you're bringing me in here." He couldn't carry on a conversation at that point. I kept telling him, "Don't you want to come in and sit down?" I thought that might help reconnect some tissue. But it didn't. He just smiled and walked to the back [of the room]. We had a huge work area, with cubicles for the architects. He went back there. He spent all his time with them.

That their father had a heart attack and a stroke when they were just finishing up college played a significant role in my girls' lives. They got to the point where they were afraid for anything to happen to me.

I've always believed that my stepfather, who was running Fisk as the dean, and Calvin McKissack, who was on the board of trustees, somehow got together and arranged our marriage. They were very close friends.

My husband was at Howard University while I was at Fisk. I was getting ready to go out. It was around Thanksgiving. I told Dad I was on my way out.

Leatrice McKissack in her office, 1983

"Where are you going?" he said.

I said, "Out with this guy from Texas; Powell, a good-looking guy."

He said, "Well, why are you doing that?"

I asked, "Well, why not?"

He said, "Well, what about"——he called him DeBerry.

"What about DeBerry?" I said.

"Well, he's coming home for Thanksgiving," he said.

I said, "So?"

He said, "You know, sweetheart, I really don't think you should go out."

I cannot believe I listened to my father and didn't go out. And fifteen or twenty minutes later the phone rang. It was my soon-to-be husband.

Being head of an architectural and engineering firm is not easy. It's a man's world. I tell my girls this every day—it's still a man's world. You have to learn how to fit into it; it's all about business. It's nothing personal.

If you're going to be a businessperson as an African American, you have to realize that you are going to have some hardships. You have to be totally committed.

You're going to have your peaks and your valleys. If you're not married or if you get married, make sure your spouse understands that. It's not going to be easy.

My basic philosophy is not to do harm to people. I try very hard to live by the Golden Rule, and that is, do unto others as you would have them do unto you.

Being head of an architectural and engineering firm is not easy. It's a man's world. I tell my girls this every day—it's still a man's world. You have to learn how to fit into it; it's all about business. It's nothing personal.

—LEATRICE McKISSACK

HENRY H. MITCHELL

Born in Columbus, Ohio, on September 10, 1919

Minister, educator

Selected and interviewed by
NVLP Fellow Lindsey Young, Spelman College

———————

Reverend Henry H. Mitchell is a renowned speaker and author of several books, among them Black Preaching, Soul Theology, *and* Preaching for Black Self-Esteem. *He was the director of the Ecumenical Center for Black Church Studies in Los Angeles prior to serving as dean and professor of History and Homiletics at the School of Theology at Virginia Union University. After leaving this position in 1987, Mitchell and his wife, Ella, taught together as visiting professors of homiletics at the Interdenominational Theological Center in Atlanta from 1988 to 2000.*

My father was a letter carrier and was quite active in youth programs for the church. He ran a scouting program, took us camping and hiking, and was a sponsor for the youth choir. We had a wonderful choir, and I was delighted, once my voice had changed, to sing bass.

My first recital, I sang mezzo-soprano wearing my first pair of long pants! I was in high school before I was allowed to wear long pants; little boys didn't wear long pants in those days.

Because my daddy became ill and we got in a lot of debt, my mother went into the home-baking business. I had interesting experiences as a result. I would walk down the street with a great big basket of home-baked products, which I sold from door to door. Then she added a chicken business. I would go out in the country with my cousin, [my mom's business] partner, who was not able to read. He was a marvelous fellow, but he couldn't read and write, so at age twelve I went through the countryside with him to pick out chickens at a farmer's farm and buy them. I would do all the paperwork.

On Friday night we would kill the chickens and clean them. Then, on Saturday, beginning at six thirty in the morning, I would run a stand in the public market with baked goods, poultry, eggs, and butter.

I've done a little of everything. In high school, I had the privilege of helping my mother's sister's husband. My uncle was a master electrician and a master plumber who serviced bulk stations and gasoline service stations. I got a lot of interesting experience. A deacon at church gave me an apprenticeship in carpentry.

I had done enough that when we built our first home, I handled much of the plumbing and electricity, did some of the carpentry, all the Sheetrock, and all the tile.

I grew up in a frugal-living family. It was a great place to grow up because my parents put a lot of responsibility on us.

My dad had me grinding the valves in the Model-T with a stick with a suction cup on the end when I was twelve years old. I would free up the valves and spin the valve in the valve seat. I changed the speed bands in the automatic transmission. They didn't call it that then, but later on the automatic transmissions were built on the principles of the transmission with no stick in the early Model-Ts.

My father said, "If a man made it, a man can fix it, and I'm a man." He taught me that anything broken, I could fix. I changed the gears on a strange kind of a washing machine that my mother had when I was twelve years old. She said, "Henry, fix it," and I didn't know any better, so I did.

I never entertained the idea of not being married or not having children. I enjoyed doing a lot of things with children. My father defined fatherhood for me. He did a lot of things with his boys. He loved his boys. We did a lot of hiking and camping, even before we were old enough to be Boy Scouts. We traveled a lot. When I got to be a father, I took my kids all over the United States. We camped together. We made things together. I thoroughly enjoyed all of that. Even with my grandchildren, I did the same kinds of things. There's a piece of furniture in the dining room that I made with my two little grandsons.

GORDON PARKS

Born in Fort Scott, Kansas, on November 30, 1912

Photographer, author, filmmaker, composer

———

As photographer, author, poet, filmmaker, and composer, Gordon Parks has lived the life of a thousand men. With a camera, Parks has captured history in his photographs of Vogue *models and more than three hundred* Life *magazine assignments. As a director, he has produced award-winning films including* The Learning Tree, *based on his novel; the Academy Award–winning motion picture* Shaft, *and the Emmy Award–winning documentary* Diary of a Harlem Family. *His symphony, sonatas, concertos, and a ballet about the life of Dr. Martin Luther King Jr., titled* Martin, *have been performed and recorded internationally. He has been awarded the NAACP's Spingarn Medal, the World Press Photo Award, the National Medal of the Arts, more than forty honorary degrees, and several lifetime-achievement awards. The book* Half Past Autumn: The Life Works of Gordon Parks *brings together his photographs with his work as a filmmaker, novelist, poet, and musician.*

During World War II, Parks worked as a photographer for the Office of War Information. The U.S. Armed Forces were officially segregated and remained so until President Harry Truman ordered their integration in 1948.

*M*y first assignment as a photographer in World War II was to cover the 332nd fighter group, the first black fighter group in World War II history.

I was training with them. My assignment was to photograph them in combat, then leave them, go to England, and fly over the English bomber group to show the "red tails," as they were called, escorting the bombers over to targets in Germany.

General Benjamin Davis—Colonel Davis at the time—was the head of the 332nd fighter group. He called me in one day, just days before they were supposed to go to the port of embarkation, and said, "Your papers are not in order. You can't travel with us. Something is wrong. You better go back to the Pentagon immediately and find out; otherwise you can't travel with us."

So I hopped a plane to Washington, D.C. As I was going back to the Pentagon on a bus, I met a highly decorated black pilot—Lee Rayford. He and another pilot were going to get refurbished to go back and fight the Luftwaffe. They could have stayed in training here, but they chose to go back and fight. Lee Rayford—who'd been shot down and whose uniform is full of his medals—the other pilot, and I get on the bus, along with a white major and two captains and a little black lady.

We sat down a few seats behind the bus driver, who says, "You have to go in the back."

"I what?"

"You have to go in the back. Colored people sit in the back."

The little black woman says, "Terrible."

The white major looks over, and the captain comes over to us and says, "Can you fellows move in the back, because the major has a very important appointment at the Pentagon, and he doesn't want to be late. I know how you feel, but he would appreciate it if you went back."

The bus driver says, "If you don't move back, I'm going to get the MPs and have you taken to the back."

I said, "I'll tell you, Captain. You tell the major I'm from the Office of War Information. If he wants us to move back, give me his rank and serial number."

Instead, the major said to the bus driver, "Drive on. Don't you know when you're licked? Drive on."

So the bus driver drove on. That's what we faced constantly.

When I got to the Pentagon, they told me my papers were in good shape, no problem. Somebody was working against me. Ted Poston, who was working for the Office of War Information too, said, "Don't you know what it is? It's the southern senators and congressmen. They don't want you to go over there and show these pilots doing their thing. They want you out."

On the way [back to the 332nd fighting group], I saw a boat landing in Washington with a lot of white soldiers and about five black soldiers. A black woman was getting off the boat, and the soldiers trampled her. One of the black pilots got so angry, he ran over and wanted to fight.

I told him, "You can't whip a hundred fifty soldiers. Let's get her up and get her out of the way, okay? But don't start a fight with a hundred fifty soldiers when there's only five of us. You know we can't win."

He wanted to fight anyway. Somehow I calmed him down. He thought I was an officer, and I was able to tell him to get back because I had an officer's cap on.

When I got to the camp where the pilots were, I found out they'd been

Gordon Parks as a young man, ca. 1927

having trouble, although they'd only been there two days. The white pilots would not stand in the line and eat food with them. Some of the black pilots looked like they were white, and they'd get in line, and the white pilots would get in behind them. So it got to be a joke. But there was almost gunfire one night. This was all happening as these guys were going to fight for their country.

Colonel Davis called me the day before we were supposed to leave and said, "Mr. Parks, your papers are still not in order."

I said, "Colonel Davis, don't you see what they're trying to do? Don't you understand they're just trying to pull me out of here, because they don't want your fighter pilots to get recognition from the Office of War Information?"

He's a West Pointer, and he said, "I'm sorry, there's nothing I can do about it."

I said, "Well, okay. I'm going back and resign my position."

He said, "Okay. Have a chopper take you to the airport, and that's it."

As I flew into Washington, I could only see all of the prejudice that had confronted me, and I was angry. I went to the airport to wait for my plane to New York. I was angry, and I realized I had to watch myself because I was terribly angry. And would you believe it, a white man sat down next to me. He looked like a cracker from the South. He looked exactly the way they look, and I said to myself, "If he says one word to me, I'm going to hit him."

And he did say one word to me. He said, "It's a nice day for flying, Soldier. Would you like a cigarette?"

I said, "Thank you. It *is* a nice day for flying," and I took a cigarette.

He lit it for me, and we sat there in peace. I realized how wrong I was about this man because he was white and looked like a cracker.

"It's a nice day for flying," I said to the stewardess when I got on the plane. I said to the taxi driver when I got off the plane, "It's a nice day for flying." I said that all the way into Harlem.

NORMAN MAURICE RATES

Born in Owensboro, Kentucky, on January 1, 1924

Minister, professor

Selected and interviewed by
NVLP Fellow Shayla Griffin, Spelman College

———— • ————

Over the course of his long career, Dr. Norman Maurice Rates served as college minister, professor of religion, and chair of the Department of Religion at Spelman College. He is Dean Emeritus of Sisters Chapel. His two published works are Sanctuary—The Sisters Chapel at Spelman College *and* African Women of the Bible.

I grew up in the "fear and the admonition of the Lord." We were a staunch Baptist family. We would go to Sunday school and stay for church. The minister, when I was a little boy, was a long-preaching preacher. He would preach for about two hours. We would go home after church and have dinner. Afterward we were not allowed to do too much playing. We would go back to church at about five in the afternoon for BYPU, the Baptist Young People's Union, and stay for evening service.

On Wednesdays I would go to church for prayer meetings when others did not. I don't know why. I was afraid of the Lord, so I tried to do good things to please God.

My next oldest brother, who was nothing of an angel, had a lot of influence on me in terms of religion. He told me once, "Norman, when you do something that God is displeased with, you may want to say, 'Lord, forgive me.' And then what you ought to do is to be courteous to God; after a pause, and God forgives you, God may say, 'You're forgiven.' And you say, 'Yes, sir.' "

I developed a little rhythmic pattern. "Lord, forgive me. Yes, sir. Lord, forgive me. Yes, sir." And it became so rhythmic that it became "Lord-forgive-me-yes-sir-Lord-forgive-me-yes-sir."

I had a relationship with God which I find now was not too healthy. I've learned since that it is better to have a fear of God rather than to be afraid of God. The fear of God is you want to do what pleases God; you don't want to disappoint God. Being afraid of God is not wanting to have God scold you, beat up on your conscience. Over the years, I had to develop that philosophy.

I read the Bible from "civer" to "civer" several times—that means "cover to cover"—and in reading the Bible, I always came across stories and verses that I never remembered reading before. It was always a new adventure. I was fascinated by the genealogies, where somebody begot somebody, begot somebody, begot somebody. We were using the King James version of the Bible.

When I went to church, I would listen to the preacher, the arguments, the choir, and come home and mimic those people. I had no intention of becoming a preacher.

When I came to Spelman, not only was I the college minister, I also had to teach. Over the years, as I taught, I began to develop courses that were more suited for women. When I came here, my two courses were *Old Testament Literature and History* and *The Life of Christ.* Eventually it dawned on me, "I'm teaching women, yet I'm teaching women from a male perspective." I had already had a taste of religion taught by white teachers from a white perspective. I said, "I should be more sensitive to the needs of women."

I first developed a course called *Women of the Bible.* And in teaching that course, I emphasized that the women in the Bible are its backbones. They are the people in the background who nevertheless are the stronger of the male characters in the forefront. I taught the Bible not from a woman's perspective, because I am not a woman; I taught it projecting the significant role of women in the Bible. I hope I met some of the needs of women to see themselves in a position other than subservient to men. We know religion as highly patriarchal.

I also began to teach courses that dealt with society, Christian thought, themes that were relevant to the times, making them very practical. I'm disturbed that a man can be put in prison for life for having drugs, but another man can steal billions of dollars from a corporation and can get out on parole. These inequities disturb me.

I don't think that the black male is lost. The picture is not as bad as some say, but it's bad enough, and the church needs to step in and do something about it. The black church has failed the black male. Maybe it has failed because it has rescued the black female. Some congregations are overwhelmingly female. Men are few in numbers. They're the ones in charge. The men are the leaders. But the supporters are the masses of black women. We need to reclaim the churches' black male. We need service-oriented programs to rescue black men. Black Muslims have done an excellent job in reclaiming black men. They've done a better job than our black churches.

So I am a critic of formal religion. I'm searching for wisdom every day. I don't know that I have much wisdom. I just try to live my philosophy rather than to articulate it: respect for women, respect for all people, that everyone is a child of God, and therefore we should treat everyone as a child of God. I don't think God favors one race, one religion. I would like for people to be more respectful of the beliefs of others. Humankind is not lost, but we have a lot of recovering to do. When I look at the suffering of people throughout the world, I don't believe God is on our side. We should strive to be sure that we're on God's side.

I don't think that the black male is lost. The picture is not as bad as some say, but it's bad enough, and the church needs to step in and do something about it. The black church has failed the black male.

—NORMAN MAURICE RATES

FRED SHUTTLESWORTH

Born in Montgomery County, Alabama, on March 18, 1922

Minister, activist

The Rev. Fred Shuttlesworth, currently the pastor of the Greater New Light Baptist Church in Cincinnati, Ohio, is one of the giants of the American Civil Rights Movement. He is generally regarded, along with Dr. Martin Luther King Jr. and Rev. Ralph Abernathy, as one of the movement's "big three."

Raised in Birmingham, Alabama, he served between 1953 and 1961 as pastor of Birmingham's Bethel Baptist Church and organized the Alabama Christian Movement for Human Rights. In 1957 he was also one of the five organizers of the Southern Christian Leadership Conference (SCLC) with Dr. Martin Luther King Jr., and later helped the Congress of Racial Equality (CORE) organize its "freedom rides" campaign.

During the civil rights struggles in Birmingham, Rev. Shuttlesworth's house was a frequent target of bombing attacks, and he was hospitalized after a fire hose slammed him against a building during a civil rights demonstration. Having been jailed more than twenty-five times for his civil rights activities, he remained determined to see the Birmingham struggle end in victory. A founding board member of the Birmingham Civil Rights Institute, he makes frequent trips not only to Birmingham but also to other areas around the country to speak of the lessons learned in Birmingham.

He is the subject of a 1999 biography by Andrew M. Manis, A Fire You Can't Put Out: The Civil Rights Life of Birmingham's Reverend Fred Shuttlesworth *(University of Alabama Press).*

It was Christmas Eve night, 1956, when my home was bombed. My deacon, Charlie, always came on that night. We were talking in one room. My wife, his wife, and the four children were in the other room.

It's an amazing thing. I had preached that Saturday, and I said a prophetic word. I said, "Do you know I expect any day for some Klansman to throw a stick of dynamite at my house."

It turns out they had put the dynamite in the space between the brick church and the frame house. Sixteen sticks of dynamite went off around about nine something that night. The whole corner of the house, including the roof, was blown off.

The wall that was between my head and the dynamite was shattered; the house was now leaning. I couldn't go out the front. The floor was blown out from under my bed. Charlie got out of the back with my wife and children.

Now, you know what I was thinking about when that bomb went off? We had made a promise to ride the buses. That was in my mind, and further than that was the psalm when David said, "The Lord is my light and my salvation. My enemies came upon me to eat up my prey. They stumble in fear."

Strange thing, I knew I wouldn't be hurt. I felt more ecstatic at the time that bomb went off, because I knew it was meant for me. But God has ways of undoing what evil men do. But it's for a purpose. He saved me to lead the fight. The people say that. I knew that I wasn't alone. I have never felt more comforted in my life.

[Hours later, my wife and I were leaving the police station] and here was a big, burly policeman. He was almost a head taller than me, and large. He was waiting, I guess, to see what I looked like.

He didn't say anything, he just looked at me, took his cap off, and took a hankie out of his pocket and rubbed his head. He never said a word, just looked at me for about thirty seconds. When I saw him, I just stopped. Then he put his cap on and walked toward the door, getting closer to the tremendous crowd outside. [Then he stopped and] kind of shook himself, shook his head, and for the first time he spoke to me. He said, "Reverend, I'm so sorry. I'm really sorry." He said, "I know these people, and I didn't think they would go this far." Then he took about three steps, turned around, and stopped. I stopped too. I hadn't said one word to him. He said, "Reverend, I tell you what I would do if I were you. I would get out of town as quick as I could." This was the first time I spoke. I said, "Well, officer, you're not me." I said, "You go back and tell your Klan brethren that if God could keep me through all of this, I'm here for the duration. And the war is just beginning."

He didn't answer me, but went on to the crowd. I went and got into my car, and my baby daughter came and got in my lap, looked up at me, and said, "They can't kill us, can they, Daddy?" I said, "No, baby, they can't kill hope."

It's an amazing thing. I did not expect to live to get forty years old in the Deep South. I expected to get killed. Martin, all of them, expected me to get killed in Birmingham before anybody else. And then here I am, "double forty" and still going.

Martin Luther King was God's spokesman to the country. His task was not mine. I'm a battlefield-type general. I lead troops to the battle. Sometimes Martin had to be pushed; he was very slow. He agonized. One of his problems was that he hated to hurt people's feelings. The first time I met King was in 1954. The town was agog with him coming. When he got to Birmingham, he wanted to meet me. I was the one that was pushing up dust in Birmingham, and he came over. We both agreed that segregation was wrong, and that the black population especially had been debilitated by not having opportunities. We agreed that something ought to be done.

In some of the letters I wrote him later, I told him that good speeches don't make good action. I think he grew into what he had to do. We were different people. I respected him. People right now say, well, Martin felt this way about me. I don't give a slap happy about what anybody thought about me. I don't in my church right now; I tell them the world is my pulpit. I think people ought to live that way. I think people ought to be more committed to what they are, what they say.

People have stopped far from the line of justice and equality and freedom in this country. So whenever I speak, I'm urging folks to do something. See, I tell people I haven't been to jail in a long time, and I'm kind of getting the jailhouse itch. Let's start something. Let's do something. I pray for the church because we aren't saying certain things. See, the church ought to now be talking about the war. It ought to be talking about medicine for the poor. I never thought I should pull back; even today I don't think I should pull back.

I wish people could rally now, because we aren't near reaching freedom and justice. Justice is what we need. People forget that God is a God of both mercy *and* justice. I doubt if you've heard a sermon on justice from anybody in a long time.

We preach half of God. That's why the world is like it is. We've got to move a little bit more toward spirituality, acknowledgment of God for all of His goodness. [The attack on] the World Trade Towers was designed to sort of humble us a little bit. Well, we humbled for a moment; everybody filled the churches up for a while.

But now [President] Bush wants to act like a cowboy, "dead or alive"; you don't talk like that. That's a good movie, but not the American psyche. It shocks me to hear [Defense Secretary Donald] Rumsfeld talking about killing, killing, killing. That isn't our psyche. But we are killing each other psychologically and otherwise by what we do in this country. The reason I don't despair is that I know there's a plan for my life, just like there's one for yours. It's impossible for us to know. I was telling a friend a while ago that there is belief, faith, and trust. Trust is the highest. When you get to where you trust God, you don't doubt anything. That's where you get rid of all fear.

I pray for the church because we aren't saying certain things. See, the church ought to now be talking about the war. It ought to be talking about medicine for the poor.

—FRED SHUTTLESWORTH

PERCY SUTTON

Born in San Antonio, Texas, on November 24, 1920

Attorney, media industry leader, politician, activist

———————

Percy Ellis Sutton is the youngest of fifteen children of Samuel J. and Lillian Sutton, both educators who were determined to provide for their children the best opportunities possible. Sutton attended three historically black colleges: Prairie View Agricultural and Mechanical College in Texas, Tuskegee Institute in Alabama, and Hampton Institute in Virginia. He also attended Columbia University, and graduated from Brooklyn Law School.

He learned to fly, and earned money as a stunt pilot at county fairs. In World War II he served with the famous Tuskegee Airmen, winning combat stars as an intelligence officer.

He set up a law firm in Harlem that handled many cases free of charge, including those of more than two hundred defendants in 1963 and 1964, during massive arrests of civil rights workers in the South. Sutton served as a consultant to the Student Nonviolent Coordinating Committee, and was for many years the attorney for Malcolm X.

As a New York State assemblyman, Sutton was a major supporter of state funding to build the New York Public Library's Schomburg Center for Research in Black Culture, and also of the Search for Education, Elevation, and Knowledge (SEEK) program, which enabled promising students from disadvantaged backgrounds to enter college. He served as Manhattan Borough President from 1966 through 1977.

In 1971, Sutton became the owner and CEO of the Inner City Broadcasting Corporation, and began purchasing black-owned media businesses, among them radio station WLIB-AM, the first black-owned station in New York City. He was legal adviser, fund-raiser, and confidant to Rev. Jesse Jackson in his 1984 and 1988 presidential campaigns. His corporation recently purchased and restored the Apollo Theater, a Harlem landmark.

Sutton has received countless awards, among them the NAACP's Spingarn Medal.

I urge people to intern, work for nothing. That's what I did in my earlier days. I worked for nothing because I wanted to learn. After you've learned, think about whether or not you are willing to put some of your own money in the business you want to develop or you can impress someone to lend you money. This era we're living in now is long past a class-industrial society. We're in the latter days of a high-technology society. You need to be very smart and have great access. And after you've learned everything there is to know, you've got to be willing to invest in yourself. So take a job. Become an intern. Then invest some money in yourself, and start a business.

Be prepared the day you start to fall on your face. Then get up, wipe your face, dust off your knees, and start again.

I never think about personal, individual wealth. I know when I [have a specific] need for money—when the IRS people come after me, or when the people who lost money want to be paid. But I believe that the future of black people has to be the accumulation of wealth, and passing that wealth along.

At one time I wanted to make Inner City a vehicle to improve conditions for a lot of people; I wanted to take it public.

If I had to start it over again, I would do a family thing, not bring in anybody. For the most part, I've brought people in to various things I've done because I wanted to help them, not because I thought they could help me. I would never do that again. I would assemble my nieces and nephews and assign each of them to build a structure that cares about people. I'd say, "Here's what I want you to do in the next generation. If you don't like it, get out." I believe in conserving wealth, discovering methods by which one can conserve money and pass it on to new generations.

Our greatest opportunities for success are in the political and in the economic arena, if we can join together and if we're not afraid to build a structure that involves both politicians and [financiers]. We can build structures that teach our people at the bottom of the ladder how to participate; and [where] everybody who graduates from a college or gets a good job is obligated to revisit their community and to contribute to it. They have an obligation to furnish the opportunity they received to everybody else.

I hope everybody feels as I do about this multigenerational wealth. Apples didn't throw apples from the trees of power. Protest brought those apples down. Change did not come except by an aggressive approach. People shook the apple trees. We apples have an obligation to help others.

I'm an old man who's lived a good life. I came from a nurturing family. I had a father and a mother who did everything they could to make me be-

Percy Sutton as a Tuskegee Airman

lieve that America would be one day kinder to me than it was to them and my ancestors. I am an observer of black progress in America, and I am disturbed when I see some making progress and not caring what happens to the rest of us. I've been hurt many times in my efforts. I get angry. I know I cannot stay angry, because anger closes doors. I was taught that. I did not always practice that, but I do now, as I've gotten older. I've learned to control my anger.

I've fought for access, and now have access to power, access to entities of progress. And I still care about people. I help people. (It is wearing me thin right now because many people who helped me when I started have grandchildren now, and the grandchildren call on me!) Leadership means having followers. The best ways to evaluate whether you're truly a leader is to measure what kind of organization you built and how many people you influence.

At this stage of my life, I am happiest when I'm where we are sitting right now, on this farm, raising peaches, plums, apples, and cherries. Except this was not a good year. The frost came on April the 12th. The trees were frozen at twelve degrees. All the fruit was wiped out, all of my food. I have some vegetables, tomatoes and other things, that are coming along. I hope to harvest some vegetables.

The older I get, I still say, no matter how well you do, don't forget the obligation you have to your community. Help other people. Involve yourself in your community. It's tiring. It's costly sometimes. I could be on Park Avenue, where my son is, but my office is on 125th Street. When I leave West 135th Street, where I live, and go to 361 West 125th Street, next door to the post office, most of the people I see don't want anything from me. They introduce their children to me. I'm introduced as Malcolm's attorney, as Jesse's attorney, or as former borough president. Some of the things they remember are not pleasant for me, but they don't see it that way, and they'll say, "God bless you. God bless you, Percy Sutton." That's the most satisfying thing. Nothing else is as important.

I get angry. I know I cannot stay angry, because anger closes doors. I was taught that. I did not always practice that, but I do now.

—PERCY SUTTON

EDWARD S. TEMPLE

Born in Harrisburg, Pennsylvania, on September 20, 1927

Retired coach

Selected and interviewed by
NVLP Fellow Kenneth Thompson, Fisk University

—◆—

Born in Harrisburg, Pennsylvania, on September 20, 1927, Edward S. Temple was an all-city athlete in basketball, football, and track at John Harris High School. After graduation he attended Tennessee State University, where he earned a B.A. and M.A. in health and physical education. During his junior year of college, he met his future wife, and they married the following year. The summer after his senior year, Temple became the head coach for the women's track team at Tennessee State, a position he would hold for forty-four years.

Temple began his coaching career with three runners and a budget of $150. In the first year the team competed in one meet. He went on to coach three U.S. Women's Olympic Track Teams, the Pan American Games in 1959 and 1975, and the U.S. team in its 1975 competition against China. All along, he continued to coach the women's track team at Tennessee State, from which forty women went on to win twenty-three Olympic Medals.

*J*n Pennsylvania we didn't have formal segregation in the schools, but segregation was still a reality. I was the only black on the basketball team. Three or four were on the football team. Four or five were on the track team. But we were way in the minority.

When we played football games in Hershey, Pennsylvania, the cheerleaders cheered, "Get that nigger." This was in Hershey, Pennsylvania, where the Hershey bars and everything chocolate are made. When we played football in Shamokin, Pennsylvania, one of the coal mine towns, they would count, "One, two, three," as we got off the bus, and when they'd counted every black person who came off the bus, they'd holler, "Eight niggers on the team." I'd hear it go right down the block. "Eight niggers on the team."

You would think this would happen in Tennessee or Mississippi, but it happened in Pennsylvania, too. In the forties, there was a whole lot of this in Pennsylvania.

We were playing against York, Pennsylvania, and a white boy scored a touchdown by catching the ball over a black player on York's team. He ran back in the huddle and said, "Did you see me catch that ball over that nigger's head?"

He suddenly sees the three or four of us "niggers" on his team there in the huddle, and looks up and tells us, "Oh, I didn't mean you. I didn't mean you." That's the kind of stuff we lived with.

But coming to Tennessee was the first time I ran into legal segregation. Coming on the train. In Cincinnati you had to change trains. From Harrisburg to Cincinnati, you could ride anyplace you wanted to ride, but when you got to Cincinnati, blacks had to ride in a separate car. We had to sit up near the engine, which was noisy, threw off smoke and everything. As we moved on down the line from Cincinnati, I found out what segregation really was.

When I arrived in Nashville for college, I had my first black teacher. All through school, I never had a black teacher. From elementary on up, I never had more than two blacks in any classroom. My graduation class of three hundred plus had four blacks. I didn't come in contact with too many. Everything in college was black, the Tuskegee relays and so forth.

What gripes me about so many of the black athletes going to pro football and pro basketball today is they don't have an education. Of all those in school who play, very few make it to the pros. Another small percentage stays over two years; a smaller percentage stays over five years. Who stays ten years is an even lower statistic.

If you don't go to school and get an education, after your season's over, you'll be standing down on the corner with your bottle of wine saying, "I played before a hundred thousand people." You ain't accomplished nothing.

I think less of athletes like them than I do of the person who didn't have an opportunity. When he is sitting down there with that bottle of wine, at least he can say, "I would have made something of myself if I had had the opportunity." These athletes had the opportunity. They've put all their eggs in one basket. When that basket sinks, they sink.

Jayme Coleman Williams and McDonald Williams

Jayme Coleman, born in Louisville, Kentucky, on December 15, 1918

McDonald Williams, born in Pittsburgh, Pennsylvania,

on November 13, 1917

Educators

Selected an interviewed by

NVLP Fellow Crystal DeGregory, Fisk University

───◆───

Married in 1943, Jayme Coleman and McDonald Williams have dedicated their lives to teaching, civic activism, and the church. Dr. Jayme Coleman Williams's teaching career spans almost fifty years, the last fourteen of which she spent serving as the head of the Department of Communications at Tennessee State University. In 1984 she assumed the editorship of the AME Church Review, *the oldest black journal in America, becoming the first woman to be elected as a major general officer in the 197-year history of the AME Church.*

Dr. McDonald Williams taught English at various colleges and universities for forty-six years and is credited with the development and expansion of the University Honors Program at Tennessee State University, which he directed for twenty-two years. He also served as vice chairman of the Steward Board at the St. John's AME Church and still consults for the Commission on Higher Education. In tandem, the Williamses coedited the 1970 publication The Negro Speaks: The Rhetoric of Contemporary Black Leaders. *Working together throughout their careers, the Williamses have been corecipients of numerous awards, including the 2002 Joe Kraft Humanitarianism Award, granted by the Community Foundation.*

*D*R. COLEMAN WILLIAMS: This weekend we're going to Baltimore to celebrate the fiftieth anniversary of one of our students, who got married in our home and later became a bishop in the church. Mac acted as father of the bride and I as mother of the bride because they're from Bermuda and their parents were not there. Our daughter was the flower girl. We have all been commanded to come to Baltimore for this big celebration.

DR. M. WILLIAMS: People say opposites attract. To me that doesn't make sense. Based on my own experience, if two people are going to have a good marriage, they've got to be as much alike as possible. We are both religious. We both stress education. We have similar ideas about entertainment and family values—I have to use the phrase "family values"; it has a bad connotation because of right-wing people. Couples who are as much alike as possible in terms of upbringing, background, and what they want out of life have a better chance of success. I have seen some marriages crumble over money, family, religion, politics, you name it. These have never been issues for us.

DR. COLEMAN WILLIAMS: Also, people don't feel it is important to try to make things work. People go into marriage now thinking, if it works, fine, if not, I'll just divorce. You have to work at making anything good: you work at having a good marriage. Many people today are unwilling to do that.

Part of that is because young women now have such outstanding careers. They are very independent, so they are not willing to give and take like we used to be. That is unfortunate. I think once you make a commitment to someone you ought to be willing to try to make it work.

One of our young friends called me and said that she and her husband were thinking about getting a divorce and wanted to come and talk to me. I said, "Oh, no, no, no. You're not going to get a divorce. I'm simply not going to have that." They laugh now and say, "Well, you said we couldn't get a divorce."

More people need to be encouraged to try to make it work. You don't run when something is not right.

And I agree with Mac that the more alike you are, the better. People are always asking us how we find so much to talk about. They rarely see one of us without the other. We do everything together. It's been a together thing with us through the years. In fact, three of the honors we've gotten in Nashville were given to us as a couple. That picture there was given to us when we were honored by the National Conference of Christians and Jews. It was the first time they'd ever honored a husband and wife. St. Bernard Academy gave us the Otis Floyd Education Award for our humanitarian efforts in the community. We're a team, and it's been wonderful.

ANDREW YOUNG

Born in New Orleans, Louisiana, on March 12, 1932

Minister, former mayor of Atlanta, U.S. Ambassador
to the United Nations, U.S. Congressman

———— ◆ ————

Andrew Young served on the forefront of the civil rights battleground. He marched through the streets of Birmingham and Selma with his friend Martin Luther King Jr., and he was with Dr. King when he was assassinated. Though brutally beaten as he led peaceful marchers through a Florida town, Young's commitment to nonviolence never allowed him to consider fighting back.

In the early 1970s Rev. Young became the first black person from the South elected to Congress since Reconstruction. He served as U.S. Ambassador to the United Nations from 1977 to 1979 and spoke out forcefully on such issues as apartheid in South Africa as well as human rights violations and racism in the United States.

In 1981 Young was elected mayor of Atlanta. Among his most notable accomplishments was leading the successful campaign to bring the Olympics to Atlanta in 1996. As pastor of a major Atlanta church, he focuses much of his attention on facilitating economic empowerment programs both in the United States and abroad, particularly in Africa.

I never could keep still in school. I could never pay attention. If they had the understanding they have now, I would have been diagnosed as having attention deficit disorder. I still can't read without a highlighter. I was probably slightly dyslexic. I didn't do well in school and I didn't get along with teachers. I was always talking back, asking questions, and challenging authority. All of those things that contributed to my leadership ability made me a bad student.

I went to school very early. I was at Howard at sixteen, as a sophomore. The war veterans were just coming back, so a lot of my buddies were in their late twenties and early thirties. It was important to me to try to keep up. It was more important to get along with the boys and the girls than the teachers. Leadership comes not from the establishment and the status quo but from the peer group. I was developing leadership skills, both in high school and college, but not from books.

Poverty is an ignorant choice for a society such as ours. Racism, whether in welfare communities, in skinheads and hate crimes, is all poverty. Martin Luther King said, "A society cannot survive with people isolated on lonely islands of poverty in the midst of this ocean of material wealth." That's almost identical to Lincoln saying that we cannot continue to survive half slave and half free.

Nobody would defend slavery nowadays, 150 years later. In another twenty-five years, I hope we will feel the same way about poverty. We will realize that poverty is as primitive in a civilized society as human sacrifice. In fact, poverty *is* human sacrifice. It is obscene and immoral, and no intelligent people as rich as we are ought to be associated with poverty. It's too cheap and inexpensive to educate people and to house them.

I never take a relationship with a kid for granted. Anything can be something special to a kid. I remember the teachers who complimented me: there weren't that many of them. I remember the coaches who took time to teach me particular skills, the preachers and the political leaders who said a few encouraging words. I almost feel guilty when I give advice, compliments, and encouragement because it is like putting money in the bank. I know I'm investing in leadership. How much of it will pay off, you never know, but you make a lot of investments and the return is always surprising.

My grandmama used to quote the verse: "Cast your bread on the water and one day it will return." She had six children of her own. She wasn't sure whether she raised eleven or thirteen, because some of the "family" didn't stay that long. Likewise, it's hard for me to count the kids who have been through our house. But when we lived in New York and worked with the National Council of Churches, our home was a place where anybody coming from the South to the North could hang out. Sometimes they stayed for a week or two. A couple of them stayed for as long as two years. [Back in Atlanta] a kid from Tanzania came to run track at Georgia Tech, and they didn't have a place for him in the dormitory. The coach called and asked if he could stay with me for a week or so until a place opened up. I said sure. I think he stayed three years—and became a part of our family.

Any kid, no matter where they're born, who wants an education and is willing to work, should get help. All I want in return is, when they're able, they help someone else. It's simple.

We've never had any money. The top salary for the mayor of Atlanta was $50,000 a year when I was mayor, and I had three kids in college. My

Andrew Young, congressman from Georgia, ca. 1973

wife worked. But we never wanted for a thing. Again, my grandparents used to quote scripture: "I've never seen the righteous forsaken nor their seed begging bread." Whatever we needed, it always came.

Andrea was in law school, at Georgetown. Paula was at Duke. Lisa was at Howard. Lisa worked her way through engineering school. Andrea got a scholarship from the Legal Defense Fund and I only had to struggle with Paula's tuition at Duke.

Paula decided to go to Uganda with Habitat for Humanity when Uganda was still a pretty shaky place. Andrea left Georgetown Law School with a great job at Merrill Lynch in the general counsel's office. I said to her, "If you want to do something to help poor people, learn about money and how to get some money to some poor folk in Africa." She instead came down to

Georgia, and worked on capital punishment cases on death row. That wasn't what I had in mind for her.

We always want to protect our own children. I wanted them to make some intelligent choices, and they did. But I wanted them to make safe choices. I thought, "I've run enough risks for the family. Let them enjoy life." I have learned better. We always want to deprive our children of the very suffering that has made us strong. My parents pleaded with me not to go to work with Martin Luther King. I had a job in New York. We'd bought a house in Long Island. They didn't like it at all that I came back to Georgia. They were part of the New Orleans black bourgeoisie, and all of their friends called from all over, Alabama and Georgia, and said, "Please don't let Andrew get hooked up with those fellows."

Remember, the NAACP, which was part of my father's tradition and my mother's, had been teaching people that if we change the laws, people will obey the laws, and society will change. All of a sudden, we were saying, "That's too slow. We're going to *break* laws. We're going to practice civil disobedience." That was real hard for Roy Wilkins and Thurgood Marshall, whom I loved and admired. But it was a sea change, and my parents were of the Thurgood Marshall generation.

I love the blues. "Meet Me, Baby with Your Black Drawers On." That's classic New Orleans blues. "Rock me, pretty mama, rock me in your big, brass bed. Rock me until my cheeks turn cherry red."

That's what I grew up on and what my mother and my father didn't want me to play, but that was New Orleans. And that was real. I was not going to let the European tradition of the Congregational Christian Church make me sacrifice my black heritage from Louisiana. I insisted in my ordination as minister that that be reconciled. There's a good theological basis for that, too.

In the Book of Galatians, one of the issues that Paul deals with is, does a Christian have to first be a good Jew. And Paul says no. Each Christian can express Christianity in the context of their own heritage. Roman Christians can express Christianity in the context of their Roman heritage, Greek Christians in their Grecian culture. Early Christians didn't have to be Jews.

That means I don't have to act white to be a Christian. I don't have to act any way. I can express my faith in the context of the culture that I find most comforting.

I know there are some in the church who would say, "Now, Reverend, that's not the kind of music or the kind of thing we should be concerned with." I struggled in seminary to deal with all of these questions intellectually. Christianity doesn't require you to deny your sensuality, particularly in the African tradition, where sensuality and bodily movements are so much an expression of life and faith. God doesn't just love a part of me. This has very good scriptural basis. I love life. I love all of it. I love to dance. That's very African.

When I first started going to Africa, one of the things that always disturbed me was that the intellectual Africans would keep still and let the poor folk dance. One of my early visits to Africa was with Congresswoman Patricia Schroeder. The people were out there dancing, and all of the dignitaries were standing up there. Pat and I were standing there patting our feet. Finally we both got out there with the people. Then we started pulling these government officials and they were very, very embarrassed at hanging loose a little bit.

Look at Nelson Mandela. You start a drum and Mandela moves. That's an authentic African tradition, which we never really lost. In New Orleans it's a part of our funeral ceremonies. People dance back from the funeral. Whenever I die, wherever it is, I want a New Orleans band to be there and I want people to dance back from the grave and say, "Yeah, he did it all."

NVLP MISSION STATEMENT

The National Visionary Leadership Project, a nonprofit organization founded by Dr. Camille O. Cosby and Emmy Award–winning former network journalist Renee Poussaint, unites generations of African Americans, both elders and young people, in an exciting venture. They are working together to tell, preserve, and disseminate worldwide the first-person stories of their past, while creating a strong educational foundation for the young, vibrant leaders of the future.

The project includes an annual intergenerational leadership training conference, state-of-the-art website, accredited independent-study courses (most at historically black colleges and universities), and the establishment of an unprecedented collection of videotaped biographical interviews with extraordinary African American elders.

Some of these living legends (all of them at least seventy years of age) are known nationwide. Others are known primarily in their local communities and are chosen by African American college students from those communities. NVLP works with college faculty members at participating educational institutions to provide selected students with the resources to conduct extensive videotaped interviews with the community elder they've chosen. These participating institutions include Central State University, Fisk University, Howard University, Nyack College, Prairie View A&M

University, Spelman College, Wesleyan University, and West Chester University.

• • •

All of this invaluable material is placed on the NVLP website, providing worldwide access to pivotal African American autobiographical narratives and providing a whole new understanding of this country's past and the lessons to be learned from it.

The National Visionary Leadership Project . . . a permanent, intergenerational legacy of excellence. Join us at www.visionaryproject.com.

ARCHIVAL PHOTO CREDITS

177   DOROTHY HEIGHT Courtesy of Dorothy Height/National Council of
      Negro Women
187   GEOFFREY HOLDER Courtesy of Geoffrey Holder
201   JOHN H. JOHNSON Courtesy of John H. Johnson
221   CORETTA SCOTT KING Courtesy of Coretta Scott King/The King Center
233   LEATRICE McKISSACK Courtesy of Leatrice McKissack
242   GORDON PARKS Courtesy of Gordon Parks
258   PERCY SUTTON Courtesy of Percy Sutton
270   ANDREW YOUNG Library of Congress, Prints and Photographs Division

ABOUT THE EDITORS

CAMILLE O. COSBY is a producer and educator. She and Judith Rutherford James produced the Tony Award–nominated *Having Our Say* on Broadway and for television, for which it received the 1999 Peabody Award. She has also served as executive producer of numerous film projects, especially documentaries, including *Ennis' Gift, No Dreams Deferred,* and *Sylvia's Path.* She received a doctoral degree in education from the University of Massachusetts at Amherst.

RENEE POUSSAINT is a veteran network journalist and winner of three national Emmy Awards. She is the president and CEO of Wisdom Works, Inc., a major documentary production company, and a senior fellow at the University of Maryland's Academy of Leadership. She holds a master's degree in African studies from UCLA.

Proceeds from *A Wealth of Wisdom* will be used to support the National Visionary Leadership Project, a nonprofit organization.

Website: www.visionaryproject.com